High-Performance Mustang BUILDER'S GUIDE 1994-2004

SEAN HYLAND

CarTech®

Edited by: Travis Thompson

ISBN-13 978-1-932494-10-5
ISBN-10 1-932494-10-3

Item No. SA106

Printed in China

CarTech®

39966 Grand Avenue
North Branch, MN 55056
Telephone (651) 277-1200 • (800) 551-4754 • Fax: (651) 277-1203
www.cartechbooks.com

OVERSEAS DISTRIBUTION BY:

Brooklands Books Ltd.
P.O. Box 146, Cobham, Surrey, KT11 1LG, England
Telephone 01932 865051 • Fax 01932 868803
www.brooklands-books.com

Brooklands Books Aus.
3/37-39 Green Street, Banksmeadow, NSW 2019, Australia
Telephone 2 9695 7055 • Fax 2 9695 7355

Cover:
This '00 Mustang GT was a project car for the television show Sports Car Revolution. We showcased the Mustang GT as a multi-use sports car, capable of being a daily driver, weekend drag racer, and open track toy.

Title Page:
If you like running your Mustang at open-track events, suspension, brake, wheel-and-tire, and safety upgrades will probably interest you. But of course, everybody wants more horsepower.

Back Cover:

Top:
There are many types of drag racing to be involved in, from local bracket-racing and fun days to professional national events. The drag strip is the Mustang's bread-and-butter, but with some gears and sticky tires, even otherwise stock Mustangs come into their own.

Middle:
The Grand American Road Racing, or Grand Am, series events take place at famous tracks like Daytona and Watkins Glen. These three-hour races attract some of the best professional road racers.

Bottom:
Even with all this talk about building a well-rounded car, we haven't forgotten about horsepower. The engine upgrades in this book cover the 3.8L V-6, as well as 5.0L and 4.6L V-8s.

CONTENTS

Acknowledgments 4
About the Author 4
Introduction 5

Chapter 1: The Platform 6
Subframe Connectors 7
Strut Tower Braces 8
Roll Bars/Cages 8
Seam Welding 10

Chapter 2: Wheels and Tires 11
Drag Tires 15
Choosing Wheels 18

Chapter 3: Suspension 21
Rear Control Arms 22
IRS 23
Bumpsteer 24
Caster/Camber Plates 25
Springs 27
Tubular Crossmembers,
    Coil-Overs, & Alternate
    Suspension Systems 28
Anti-Roll Bars 28
Shocks and Struts 30
Rack and Pinions/Steering
    Shaft Kits 32

Chapter 4: Brakes 33
Brake Fluid 34
Brake Lines 36
Brake Pads 36
Brake Rotors 38
Calipers and Rotors 39
Brake Cooling 41
Drag Brakes 41

Chapter 5: Engines:
    3.8L, 5.0L, & 5.8L 45
3.8L 45
5.0L 50
5.8L 56

Chapter 6:
    The Modular Years 57
2-Valve 4.6L 58
4-Valve 4.6L 62
5.4L Cobra R 67

Chapter 7: Transmissions 69
T-5 5-Speed 69
T-45 and T-3650 5-Speeds 70
T-56 6-Speed 70
Aftermarket
    Transmissions 71
Shifters .71
Clutch and Flywheel 71
Automatic Transmissions 73
Transmission Mounts 75
Speedometer Calibration 75

Chapter 8: Rear Axles 76
Axle Ratios 76
Gear Installation Tips 77
Differentials 78
Axle Shafts 81
Fluid Coolers 82
Driveshafts 84

Chapter 9: Aerodynamics 85
Front Splitters 87
Rear Wings 89
Drag Cars 90
High-Speed Mustangs 91
Ride Height 91

Chapter 10:
    Safety Equipment 94
Seats 94
Seat Belts 98
Helmets 100
Steering Wheel 102
Driver's Suit 103
Fire System 103

Chapter 11: Get Involved! 104
MCA – Mustang Club
    of America 104
Fun Ford Weekend 104
NMRA – National Mustang
    Racers Association 105
WFC – World Ford
    Challenge 105
SCCA – Sports Car Club
    of America 106
Grand Am – Grand American
    Road Racing 107
NASA – National Auto
    Sport Association 107
Targa 108
Silver State Challenge 109
SCTA – Southern California
Timing Association 109

Chapter 12:
    Project Car Build Ups 110
Open-Track '99 Cobra 110
Street Racer '96 Cobra 112
Street/Show '03 Cobra 114
'00 GT Daily Driver 116
'01 Mustang Targa Car 118

Appendix A: Source Guide 121
Appendix B: Glossary 126

I would like to thank all my friends and family, for the constant support and feedback while I am involved on a project such as this book – and also juggling four or five other projects at the same time. Thanks also to John Mihovetz, a great sounding board on many projects, a good racer, and a great friend. Finally, thanks to all the amazing people at Sean Hyland Motorsport, who work their hearts out for me, each and every day.

About the Author

Sean Hyland has raced, wrenched, and developed Mustangs for more than half his 30 years in motorsport. Having cut his teeth in autocross and pro rally competition in the early 1980s, he moved on to be a successful driver and team owner in the Firehawk Endurance road race series in the 1990s.

As Sean became immersed in developing the 4.6L engine in the mid 1990s, time commitments forced his own motorsport adventures to take a back seat to his business, Sean Hyland Motorsport.

Sean is still at the forefront of 4.6L Modular V-8 development today, and he's justifiably proud of his achievements, most notably the 4.6L and 5.4L engine block that he designed for high-performance applications. Today, Sean is involved with making Mustangs go faster every day, and he's also the resident racing expert on Speed Channel's *Sports Car Revolution*. Sean still finds some time to spend with his wife Barb, and two growing girls, Samantha and

The Pikes Peak International Hillclimb is famous worldwide. Sean climbs the mountain in his 1996 Cobra during the 75th running of Pikes Peak in 1997.

Sean is flying high in Targa Newfoundland in 2003 aboard his 2001 Mustang with 4.6L Cobra power.

Sarah. Born in Montreal in 1958, Sean has made Woodstock, Ontario, his home for many years. Many of the procedures and practices in this book were developed and all are available at Sean Hyland Motorsport.

The decade of performance Mustangs built on the SN95 chassis represents the high water mark for enthusiasts. Never before has such a range of performance cars been available from a manufacturer – from the 5.0L '94-'95 Mustangs, through the '96-2001 4-valve Cobras, to the factory supercharged '03-'04 Cobras. The factory also built two off-the-shelf racecars, the '95 Cobra R and the 2000 Cobra R, plus specialty Mustangs like the Bullitt and Mach 1, during this period. This decade of Mustangs indeed had it all. Whatever your taste, Ford produced a Mustang for you.

For giving enthusiasts such cars, Ford has been rewarded with unrivaled loyalty. The '03-'04 Cobras even made believers out of non-Ford owners because the Mustang never forgot its performance/value roots: give the buyer performance value for their dollar, and they reward you with their business every time.

Someone told me once that the late-model Mustang is the world's best 7/8ths completed car – most Mustangs are finished by the owner to reflect his or her taste and desire. Ford has given the enthusiast a blank canvas with the Mustang, allowing each owner to modify the car according to his or her own individuality, an expression of themselves. This phenomenon is unique to North America, as most other parts of the world do not embrace the automotive culture as fervently as we do.

The purpose of this book is to celebrate the decade of the SN95 Mustang, and to provide information on preparing and modifying the 1994-2004 Mustang for improved performance on the street, drag strip, autocross, or road-race circuit. The SN95 Mustang includes all cars built between 1994 and 2004. Techniques and components required are covered in detail, in order to provide you, the reader, with the most up-to-date information possible. This book uses examples of suc-cessful Mustangs to illustrate the potential of properly built and sorted cars. Many of these cars have set records, won races and championships, and the techniques employed are just as relevant to your street car as they are to a competition car. Many of you probably already own a late-model Mustang, but some may not, so I also discuss the differences between some of the model years, to provide information that helps the reader choose the best type of car for a specific use.

The SN95 Mustang comes equipped with several different powertrain combinations, and each is covered in some detail, providing the reader with the best information possible. Building reliable power for the various types of engines used in these chassis is our primary goal. The measure of the success of this book is in how you can take this information and apply it to your car – build it to be better handling, better braking, more powerful, safer, and most of all … more fun to drive. Enjoy!

The 2003 and 2004 Cobra came with a 390-hp super-charged 4.6 DOHC. These Cobras came with a forged crank, forged rods, forged pistons, a T-56 6-speed, and independent rear suspension – what a value!

The SN95 platform is based on the old Fox-body platform. Here's Sean racing a 1988 Mustang LX at Mosport in 1990.

The Platform

The SN95 body shell improved the overall torsional rigidity over its predecessor, the original Fox-body platform. The body shell incorporates a front and rear subframe, since the Mustang is a unibody construction, without a separate frame. In 1999, the new edge Mustang incorporated a new floorpan, which again offers an improvement in chassis stiffness over the earlier SN95 body shell.

The stiffer the chassis is, the more responsive it is to suspension tuning, and the more repeatable those changes are. To that end, as cool as convertibles are, if your plan is to drag race, autocross, or road race your Mustang, and you want to have the most competitive car you can – select a coupe. Although successful competition cars have been con-

It's always handy to have a jacking point on each side to lift both the front and rear tire at the same time. A proper jacking point must be welded in place to prevent damage to the floor.

structed from convertibles, it's still better (and a lot easier) to use a coupe.

If I were building a top-flight competition car, the first thing I would do is put the car up on jack stands and check the squareness of the chassis before proceeding to prepare the chassis. Starting with the frame rails parallel to the floor, drop plumb bobs off the front and rear suspension pick-up points and make marks on the floor. In the case of the front pick-up points, hang the plumb bob through the front K member bolt hole in the frame rail, and at the rear, hang the bob off the rear lower control arm attachment point. If the lengths of your lines have discrepancies, they can be adjusted by straightening the body shell on a frame machine (if it's the

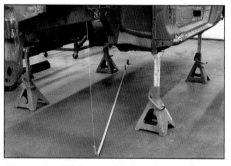

It's a good idea to look your project car over before you sink a bunch of money into it. Here, we're checking the chassis for squareness using a plumb bob and tape measure.

A jacking point can be fabricated from a 5- x 5-inch square of 3/16-inch mild-steel plate. You should also weld a 2-inch piece of 1-3/4-inch tubing to provide a secure lift point for a service jack.

result of a collision), or by grinding the holes slightly oversize and welding a mild steel plate in place to act as a washer. Once we have established square attachment points for the suspension links, we can begin stiffening the car. Production tolerances in the assembly plant sometimes stack up to create variances in the body shell dimensions. In the case of the Mustang, many of the stamping dies that formed the floorpan sections and the fixtures that held these pieces in alignment became worn over the years, and the body shells varied quite a bit from the blueprint. I know that the IRS assembly supplied to the Mustang assembly line for the '99 and '01 Cobra had to be built out of tolerance from the prints, otherwise it would not fit the body shell during assembly.

Chassis stiffening can be as simple as a set of frame connectors or as advanced as seam welding the chassis, depending on your requirements.

Subframe Connectors

The Mustang body, being of unitized construction, has no frame per se. Rather, it has front and rear subframes spot welded to the floor that adds strength and rigidity to the body shell assembly, and provides the mounting points for the suspension. Subframe connectors join the front and rear subframes with a link of rectangular or round tubing, either of which is stronger than the floorpan alone. Tying the subframes together adds torsional rigidity to the chassis and reduces the bending in the middle of the car. Just try opening the door on a convertible Mustang supported on a hoist before and after subframe connectors have been installed. The difference is dramatic.

The best type of subframe connectors feature a large area joining the connector to the subframe, and also a cross bar bolting into the front seat anchors in the floorpan. The Kenny Brown super subframe connectors are my favorite. A bolt-in subframe connector is never going to perform quite as well as a weld-in unit, simply due to the flex inherent in a bolted joint. Nonetheless, if you don't have access to welding equipment or the budget to pay someone to weld them in, a bolt-in connector is still a vast improvement over none at all, and a bolted-in connector can always be welded at a later date, further improving the stiffness of the assembly.

Kenny also has some additional items that can be added to his subframes

It is important to have the car resting on its wheels when installing subframe connectors, replicating the loads on the chassis. A drive-on hoist provides a convenient way to install the connectors while maintaining weight on the tires.

MIG welding the subframe connectors to the body shell provides a strong joint, ensuring maximum rigidity. Coat the welded areas with a zinc-rich primer following welding to restore OEM corrosion protection.

to form the Extreme Matrix System. A jacking rail, essentially a piece of 1-inch square tubing, is welded to the rocker panel pinch weld seam, and the Extreme Matrix (round tubing in a diagonal pattern) is welded between the subframe connector and the jacking rail. The resulting matrix is both rigid and strong. The welding and fitting time consumes the better part of a day, but the chassis is very stiff when completed.

One thing to remember when installing subframe connectors and the like is to only weld these items in on a drive-on lift. The wheels need to be resting on the drive-on ramps, simulating the load on the chassis while on the road. If

This car has subframe connectors, jacking rails, and the Extreme Matrix System tying the chassis together. This firms everything up and helps keep the car relatively straight, even once you start racing and making more horsepower and torque.

Strut braces keep the strut towers from deflecting under cornering loads, which changes your alignment settings. They also tie the cowl and the strut towers together, preventing cowl shake.

This '03 Cobra has a rear strut-tower brace to help stiffen up the IRS.

the chassis stiffeners are welded in while the suspension is dangling in the air, problems may occur, including doors that won't close properly and uneven fender gaps. Speaking of welding, all paint and undercoating should be ground off prior to welding, all welding should be done with a MIG welder, and the welds should be coated with a zinc-rich primer and painted after welding to prevent corrosion. Also, remove the seats, peel back the carpet, and move the wiring harness out of the way prior to welding on the underside of the car. It certainly gets hot enough underneath the floorpan to start a fire, and we don't want any of that.

Strut Tower Braces

Moving forward, the strut towers of the Mustang deflect under cornering loads, resulting in suspension geometry variation while cornering. If we were building a track car and had a roll cage, we would connect the roll cage to the strut towers with tubes, tying the front end together with the rest of the car. For a street car, using a properly designed strut brace can help minimize the chassis flex, contributing to the effectiveness of our chassis tuning. Ford fitted strut braces to the Mustang from 1994 to 1997, and then decided they were not required in 1998 and beyond, as the chassis was now rigid enough without it. Do not believe this. The requirement still exists, but someone in accounting figured out how to save a

couple of bucks.

Both Steeda and Kenny Brown make well-designed strut braces that fit well and make a measurable improvement. Strut braces are available in both mild steel and moly tubing. The front end can benefit from the stiffer material properties of the moly tubing, so the additional cost is justified. Special braces may be required for some models, such as the Bullitt, Mach 1, and '03-'04 Cobra. A three-point strut brace is always the preferred choice, because tying in the cowl helps reduce the hinge effect where the front subframe joins the firewall. A strut brace is only as effective as its attachment to the chassis, but since it's not practical to weld them in place, care needs to be exercised when bolting in a strut brace. The bolt holes do not need to be any larger than necessary for the bolts to pass through, they need to have the rough edges deburred, and although usually not supplied, a back-up plate of 1/8-inch thick mild steel helps sandwich the body steel and reduce any movement between materials where the strut brace meets the cowl.

Finally, torque the bolts to specification, and if self-locking nuts were not provided, use thread-locking compound to secure the nut to the bolt. Rear shock braces are also available from Kenny Brown for IRS Mustangs, and help tie the rear shock towers of the unibody together, although the suspension loads transmitted through the rear shock towers are nowhere near as substantial as what the front towers receive.

One other item that deserves mention is the Steeda G-Trac bar. Ford installed a tie bar beginning in 1994, joining the rear mounting points of the front crossmember together, which reduces deflection in the crossmember under hard cornering loads. The Steeda bar still offers an improvement in stiffness, mainly through a bushed link end, rather than a flattened tube design used on the OEM bar.

Roll Bars/Cages

If that's still not stiff enough for you, it's time for a roll bar. Roll bars enhance the torsional rigidity of the chassis, plus they provide the driver with roll-over protection, which gives him or her the confidence to drive as quickly as possible. We want our roll bar to be constructed of mild steel, preferably DOM (Drawn Over Mandrel) tubing.

A 3/16-inch steel backup plate installed on the underside of the floor provides additional strength to the roll-bar attachment points. The plates should be a minimum 5 x 5 inches to spread the load.

A four-point roll bar is recommended for open-track cars. If you're going to race competitively, your class may require a roll bar or cage.

This is a serious roll cage on this open-track car, capable of protecting the driver and stiffening the chassis for the best handling.

These diagonal bars across the roof area serve to protect the driver should the car flip onto a solid object, like a large rock or tree stump.

The dash bar adds rigidity to the roll cage and protects the driver against the A pillar intruding into the drivers compartment in the event of a side impact.

Moly tubing does have higher ultimate tensile strength, but it's not as ductile, and it does not deform and dissipate the energy of a crash as well as mild steel DOM. Autopower has an affordable line of bolt-in roll bars, popular with our open-track customers. For about $300, you can get a basic 4-point bolt in roll bar, and for a bit extra, you can get a cross bar suitable for attaching 5-point competition seat belts. I like to increase the size of the floor plates on the bolt-in bars from the 3-inch by 3-inch plates they come with to a larger 5-inch by 5-inch square. The plates should be constructed of 3/16-inch thick mild steel. This spreads the load over a larger sur-face, reducing the likelihood of the main hoop punching a hole through the floor during an accident. Even though these roll bars are designed to be bolted in for easy installation, welding them in provides more rigidity to the chassis. Once again, all paint, etc., should be removed prior to welding, and welded areas should be coated with a zinc-rich primer and paint after welding to prevent corrosion from weakening the welds over the course of time.

If the roll bar is bolted in, all bolts should be grade-5 quality or better, secured with thread-locking compound or nylon lock nuts. If your motorsport involvement requires a roll cage beyond

These roll-cage door bars curve outward into the space provided by the hollowed out door, providing more crush room in case of a side impact.

the basic 4- or 6-point bolt-in roll bars available commercially, a good chassis shop is required to produce a safe, legal roll cage. The FIA Appendix J regulations, available online at www.fia.com, provides specifications and drawings on acceptable practices for roll cage construction for cars competing in road-race events worldwide. This very valuable and detailed information is an excellent reference for any roll-cage project. The NHRA publishes its guidelines for drag-race roll cages in its annual rulebook, available at www.nhra.com.

Seam Welding

Seam welding is a process that stiffens the chassis by augmenting the factory spot welds with continuous welds along the sheetmetal joints that form the unibody chassis. This process may be too elaborate for a street car, but for a consistent open-track or road-racecar, seam welding is well worth the effort. Even weekend warrior open track and drag cars can benefit from selective seam welding, primarily in the torque box area and to the rocker seams and front subframe seams. By welding the chassis structure, we're adding stiffness to the suspension pick-up points, and repeatability to our suspension tuning. Adjusting the suspension on a platform that is not rigid leads to inconsistent results from adjustments – a frustrating exercise in chasing your tail.

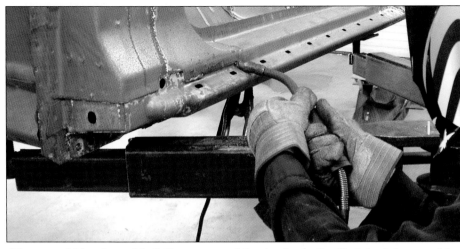

It's a good idea to weld all the seams of the body shell with 2-inch long welds separated by 1-inch spaces. This significantly improves the torsional stiffness of the chassis.

The point where the front crossmember attaches to the chassis (and where the IRS subframe attaches on the '99 and newer Cobras) also forms a location for suspension deflection to occur. If serviceability is not a prerequisite, the front crossmember can actually be welded into place, contributing to the overall stiffness of the chassis. I did this on a 1990 Mustang that we road raced, in addition to a full seam weld and roll cage. The car was so stiff that it actually carried the inside front wheel in the air on some fast corners. Whether welded

in or bolted in, the crossmember itself contributes to the stiffness of the platform. Stiffness is improved by welding the crossmember welds continuously, and plating and gusseting in selected areas. The same holds true of the rear IRS subframe on the '99-2004 Cobras, which is improved by using solid aluminum mounts connecting the subframe to the chassis.

Once we complete the chassis stiffening, we can proceed to tuning the suspension system to provide the improved performance we crave.

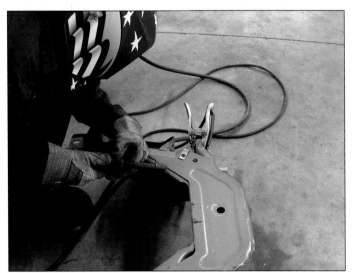

Welding the entire front crossmember enhances the front control-arm pick-up points, and contributes to a stiff chassis.

Welding the torque box structure where the lower rear control arms attach prevents the unibody from tearing apart after continuous drag-strip launches with sticky tires.

Wheels and Tires

Tires: round... black... seductive... oh, sorry, I was getting a little carried away. Changing the tires on your Mustang makes a more dramatic improvement than any other change. I'll repeat that for those of you who weren't listening – changing the tires on your car makes the single biggest improvement to the car's performance. This is important stuff! This is why if you go to the track to watch professional racing, racers are constantly changing tires. Soon after a race tire starts getting hot on the track, the performance starts to deteriorate just a tiny bit. Fresh tires are usually used for qualifying to eke out that last tenth of a second. Tires may be scrubbed in for a few laps to

The Cobra R-style wheel, first used on the 1995 Cobra R, is a popular choice with enthusiasts. The 17- x 9-inch wheel clears most aftermarket big-brake conversions. (Photo courtesy Travis Thompson)

heat cycle them, then stored away until the race, not to be used again until racing begins. If the racers run in the rain, different tires are required again, and if the track is just wet, but with no standing water, you guessed it, a different tire again. Even going from one race track to another may require changing to a tire with a different compound.

I know, you're listening to this and thinking, "Wow, if it's this complicated for racers, how am I ever going to choose a good tire for my Mustang?" Well, like most things, tires are a compromise. If you get one with excellent grip on dry roads, it may not be so good in the wet. A high-performance tire is not likely to provide good traction in the snow. Performance enthusiasts often have more than one set of tires for their car, allowing them to choose the correct tool for the job. Not everyone wants to or needs to have multiple sets of tires. Much of the decision about tires boils down to how the car is used and where you live. Obviously, if you live in the snow belt and your Mustang is your only car, you either have two sets of tires, or you live with an all-season radial, not a bad tire, but not really good at

any one particular job. On the other hand, if your Stang is a summer-only ride, you can get by with one type of tire. We are going to cover all the different options, both for street and track, summer and winter.

SN95 Mustangs came with a wide array of standard tire sizes depending on the model. Base V-6 Mustangs usually came with 15-inch wheels and 225/55/16 rubber. GT Mustangs came with 16-inch wheels and tires standard (17s were optional), while the '96-2004 Cobra rode on 17-inch rubber. The 2000 Cobra R checks in with the largest factory rubber, at 18 inches. Below is a matrix with all the standard tire sizes, along with the wheel diameter and width.

Staying with the factory wheel, we can often change the size of the tire somewhat and improve the handling performance without replacing the wheels. Tire manufacturers list wheel width ranges suitable for a particular tire they manufacture. They also list checking rim sizes (the width of rim used when the tire was developed) to determine the section width, diameter, and circumference. If we mount a tire on a rim width other than the checking width

rim, our overall diameter or section width of the mounted tire may vary from the manufacturer's specifications. Usually, this isn't a big deal, but just so you know, it can and will vary.

Most people also assume that a 245/40/17 tire is the same size from several different tire manufacturers. Wrong! For each tire size, the tire can fall within a range of dimensions as determined by the tire council. What this means for the consumer is that a particular tire size can vary by more than an inch in width between manufacturers. Certain manufacturers tend to be on the large end of the size range, while others tend to produce tires on the smaller end of the range. When you are close to the limit for clearance, this can be an important factor in deciding exactly what tires to use. The safest route to ensuring proper fitment is to consult with a wheel and tire shop that has fitted the tire/wheel combo you are considering.

Okay, so we want to upgrade our rubber, and for right now, we're going to stay with the factory rim. The following is broken down based on the type of use the Mustang is going to see.

OEM Wheel and Tire Size Chart

Year	Model	OEM Wheel Size	OEM Backspacing	OEM Tire Size
2003–'04	Cobra	17 x 9	6.12	275/40R17
2000	Cobra R	18 x 9.5	6.12	265/40R18
1996–'01	Cobra	17 x 8	5.72	245/45R17
1995	Cobra R	17 x 9	5.98	255/45R17
1994–'95	Cobra	17 x 9	5.98	255/45R17
2003–'04	Mach 1	17 x 8	5.72	245/45R17
2001–'04	GT	17 x 8	5.72	245/45R17
1994–'00	GT Optional	17 x 8	5.72	245/45R17
1994–'00	GT Standard	16 x 7.5	4.87	225/55R16
2002–'04	V-6	16 x 7.5	4.87	225/55R16
2001	V-6 Optional	16 x 7.5	4.87	225/55R16
2001	V-6 Standard	15 x 7	5	205/65R15
1994–'00	V-6	15 x 7	5	205/65R15

A: *Street Performance*

This driver wants a better tire than the original-equipment tire, and it must be capable of both good dry and wet weather performance. This driver is not going to use these tires in snow – ever. The car may see a Fun Ford drag race once a year, an MCA car show, or even do a day of open track with SVTOA, but not at an extremely competitive level. In other words, this driver needs a good all-round performer. Good tires in this class include the BFGoodrich G-Force KDW, Pirelli P Zero, and Toyo T1-R.

B: *Ultimate Street Performance*

These tires probably won't ever get hot enough on the street to fulfill their promise of ultimate grip, but this driver wants to know he/she has the best tire available for dry grip. (This driver probably does not live in rainy Seattle.) The BFGoodrich g-Force T/A KD, Toyo Proxes RA1, Yokohama Advan A032R, and Pirelli Pzero Corsa are included in this class.

C: *Weekend Warrior*

This driver engages in weekend drag racing, doesn't want to drag a second set of tires around, and may in fact also use the same tires on this daily driver for occasional non-sanctioned contests of speed when provoked by Camaro drivers. Good tires to consider are BF Goodrich Drag radials, Mickey Thompson ET Street Radials, and Nitto Drag radials.

Toyo T1-R

BFGoodrich g-Force KDW

Pirelli P Zero

BFGoodrich g-Force T/A KD

Toyo Proxes RA1

Yokohama Advan A048

Pirelli Pzero Corsa

BFGoodrich Drag Radials

Mickey Thompson ET Street Radials

Nitto Drag Radials

D: Open Track Hero

This is a second set of tires for this driver. He/she has removed their back seat in order to drag around a set of sticky R-compound tires. R-compound tires are street legal tires, developed for showroom stock road racing. Like true race tires, they do not work best until two or three laps into the race when you get some heat into the tire. R-compound tires are very soft by street car standards and have a very short lifespan. Tires in this class include Avon Tech RA, Hoosier A3505 (Autocross), Hoosier R2504 (Open Track, Racing), and Goodyear GS-CS Eagle.

Avon Tech RA

Hoosier A3S05 (Autocross)/R3S04 (Open Track/Racing)

E: Race Tires

People who run race tires change tires like most people change socks. Fresh tires are more important than food to this group of people, and nothing but the quickest track tire is sufficient. The Goodyear Eagle Sports Car Radial G-19 is included in this class.

F: Snow Tires

Say what? I know, but some folks out there drive their Mustangs year round. I have one customer with a supercharged '03 GT putting out 500 hp that's daily driven year round – and we get some serious snow here in Canada. Still, if you need to be able to get around all year, snow tires are the only way to go.

Bridgestone Blizzak

Two words: Bridgestone Blizzak. It's still the best winter tire you can get. This tire is very soft and has sipes designed to present many exposed edges to the slippery road surface, promoting grip. Blizzaks have a good self-cleaning tread design and provide excellent traction on ice, something the Northeast sees a lot of with the freeze/thaw cycle in the winter. Like all winter tires, narrower is better, so the tire can cut through deep snow and grip the solid surface beneath, not float on top and slide around. A set will last a

season, but they should be replaced every year, as the second half of the tire is nowhere near as good as the first half.

That brings me to a point I want to make about all tires. Back when I first started rally racing, I had very little money, so I began by buying used tires from other competitors, something many beginning racers do. It didn't take me long to figure out that even though I was only paying about 35 percent of new cost for a 1/2-worn tire, the first owner was definitely getting the better end of the deal. Shortly thereafter, I started buying new rally tires and selling my used ones before they lost too much tread, recovering 25 to 50 percent of my original cost. There was always a steady supply of people ready to buy good second-hand tires. The same was true when I road raced.

Tires, unlike wine, do not improve with age. Usually. Tires get hard when stored, even if they are out of the sun and in a dry, cool environment. The solvents used in producing tires continue to evaporate even after the tire is cured at the factory, and hardens with age. A natural degradation of the tire over time makes it harder and slower on the track. Usually. Once upon a time, I raced in the Firehawk Endurance Series. One of the tracks we raced at in 1990 was Mt. Tremblant in Quebec. It's a great track, lots of fun, and the cars were barely five seconds a lap slower in the rain than in the dry. The reason for this was that the surface of the track was quite abrasive, and it gave a lot of mechanical grip between the tire and the track surface. Anyway, fast forward about three years, and I've got a bunch of new, two or three year old Firestone tires at my shop that no one really wants very much – until the series goes back to Tremblant for a six-hour endurance race. Because the track surface is so abrasive, a harder tire that lasts more laps before wearing out and requiring a change has a big advantage. Vic Sifton finds out I have a bunch of these old Firestones in the size

Steel valvestems are required by some sanctioning bodies, and are recommended for any competition activities.

he uses on his Camaros and he buys them all – for cash. Anyway, aside from this isolated experience, older tires are not usually going to perform better than newer ones.

So with that in mind, if you're on a budget and need to stretch your tires to the nth degree, store them in the basement in green garbage bags over the winter. If you can afford to, get rid of them at the end of the season, and buy new tires every spring. There is usually a ready supply of people to buy the used competition tires. This of course only applies to your race or open track tires. Your everyday, street-driven perform-

ance tire is not going to be pushed to the extent that you would even know that the performance has deteriorated. That being said, storing your Mustang for the winter should involve jacking the tires off the ground, so the tires do not take a set over the winter. The nylon cords in some tires have a memory quality that retains the shape long after the tire is no longer sitting in one position anymore. This results in a lumpy tire in the spring, which is something no one wants.

Mickey Thompson ET Drag Tire. This is a full-on drag slick for track use only.

Drag Tires

Many Mustang owners drag race their cars, either on a regular basis, or a couple of times a year at special Mustang events. Some owners simply use the same tires that they use on their car everyday, but others want to take it to the next level. A drag radial tire, like the BFGoodrich g-Force T/A Drag Radial or the Mickey Thompson ET drag radial, is a DOT legal tire that performs more like a drag slick. Drag radials are made of a soft compound that gets stickier with a burnout, just like a real drag slick. The sidewall of a drag radial has less stiffness than a regular performance radial, allowing the tire to deflect on launch, helping accelerate the car, not breaking away and spinning like a stiffer tire.

A drag radial can be used on a daily driver with adequate air pressure on the street, adjusted at the track, and then driven home with correct inflation. Since drag radials are made of a softer compound, the lifespan is shorter than an average street radial, but you can still get at least a season out of a set, which isn't bad considering how good they work at the track. Drag radials have progressed to the point where racecars are now running mid 7s @ over 180 mph! A

Recommended Tire Sizes for Street Use						
1994 – '04						
	17-Inch		**18-Inch**		**19-Inch**	
	Tire	Wheel	Tire	Wheel	Tire	Wheel
Front	275/40R17	17 x 9	265/35R18	18 x 9.5	245/35R19	19 x 9
Rear	315/35R17	17 x 10.5	295/30R18	18 x 10.5	285/30R19	19 x 10
1994 – '98						
Front	255/45R17	17 x 9	245/40R18	18 x 9.5	245/35R19	19 x 9
Rear	275/40R17	17 x 9	285/35R18	18 x 10.5	285/30R19	19 x 10

Note: The wheel bolt pattern from 1994-04 is 5 x 114.3 mm (5 x 4.5 in). Always check with your wheel supplier for the manufacturer's recommended wheel offset for your application.

Some fitments may require the fender well lip to be rolled to provide additional clearance when the wheel is in bump travel.

IRS cars may need clearancing of the IRS subframe rear mount bolt when using a 315/35R17 rear fitment.

Always check for clearance between the front wheels and sway-bar when turning the steering wheel lock to lock. Additional steering rack limiter bushings will be required if there is contact or clearance is minimal.

This Mickey Thompson ET Drag slick is mounted on a 15- x 10-inch Bogart wheel. The 28- x 12-inch wide, 10.5W tire just fits in the fenderwell, with the edge of the fender rolled under.

A 15- x 3.5-inch Bogart lightweight front drag wheel is wrapped in a 26- x 7.50- x 15-inch Mickey Thomson Sportsman front tire. Having skinnys up front decreases your rolling resistance and weight.

drag radial can reduce the ET on a Mustang somewhere in the .2- to .5- second range, which is certainly the most bang per dollar you can get for a bolt-on performance upgrade. Sticky tires also make the car more consistent at the track, allowing the driver to develop his/her own skills, without the variable of inconsistent traction.

Although each tire manufacturer has different recommendations, all drag radials do respond to certain techniques. Reducing the tire pressure to 12 to 16 lbs (depending on the brand of tire) does improve the level of grip at the starting line. With such a fine line between bogging the engine and blowing off the tires (especially with the 4.6L engines, which do not have a lot of torque), the harder we can leave, the better. Drag radials also respond to a burnout – heat 'em up to get the most traction available. You don't generally want to drive through the water box at the dragstrip with drag radials. Most cars running drag radials still have the stock wide front performance tires on. The water drips out of the front tires

onto the ground when stopped at the starting line. This water then causes the rear tires to lose traction. A better plan is to drive around the water and do a dry burnout, or if you must, back into the water box. A word on drag radials and axles: I have seen stock Mustangs break the OEM 28 spline axle shafts with drag radials. Since the increased traction is enough to overload the stock axle, aftermarket 31-spline alloy axles should be factored into the budget of any Mustang using drag radials – before the car has to be towed home from the strip.

Drag slicks are the measure of a serious racer. Once you've moved up to dedicated wheels with slicks mounted on them, you are serious about drag racing. A pure drag slick from Goodyear or Mickey Thompson provides the ultimate grip at the strip. The lightweight construction of a slick, combined with the super flexible sidewall and a soft compound surface provide the maximum level of mechanical grip for forward acceleration. Mustangs with stock rear

fenderwells often use a 28 x 10.5-inch rear slick on a 15 x 8-inch wheel, or a 28 x 10.5W on a 15 x 10-inch wheel if permitted. The 10.5W is actually 12 inches wide on the tread, and is a close fit in the fenderwell. Racers who run slicks usually roll the inner fenderwell to prevent the sidewall of the tire from being cut through during a pass. Due to the growth in diameter at speed with a drag slick, radial clearance must also be checked. I've seen trim screws 1-1/2 inches away from the tire at rest show signs of tire contact after a run, so check carefully.

Slicks generally work best somewhere between 7 and 12 psi, depending on the car and track conditions. A low-pressure tire gauge is a necessity for setting tire pressure in the range we are going to be using. A proper burnout is required to get your slicks hot enough to provide maximum grip. Driving through the water box and stopping on the concrete burnout pad, a drag racer engages the line-loc, and performs a burnout, often shifting into a higher gear during the process to increase the tire speed. As the smoke begins to pour off the tires, the rubber is getting hot – reaching operating temperature. A 3- to 5-second burnout is often required on a

A quality tire pressure gauge like this Longacre unit is essential equipment for the Mustang enthusiast. Open-track cars need a high-pressure 0 to 60 psi gauge, while drag racers need a 0 to 15 psi unit. A glow-in-the-dark gauge is handy for use in the pits at night.

slick tire to reach the proper temperature. Moving the car forward a short burst before the starting line can clean the tire surface of any rubber particles driven over after the burnout. I'm always amazed by the number of racers who do a poor burnout, failing to get the tire to optimum temperature, and then spin leaving the start line. A bit of practice in developing a technique that works for your car/tire combination is a worthwhile pursuit if winning is your goal.

Cars running drag slicks usually have skinny front tires. Racers go with skinnys partially due to the reduced rolling resistance and lighter weight, but they also help at the top end of the track. The transition from accelerating to decelerating after clearing the lights at the top end of the track can be downright hairy with drag slicks on the back and wide performance radials on the front. Just imagine the car wanting to turn itself around at 130 mph. Replacing the front tires with a specific front-runner tire eliminates this tendency.

Front-runners are available in race-only models, but DOT-approved tires are also available, which are the perfect complement to ET Street rear tires. Skinnys are usually mounted on a narrow 15 x 4-inch rim, but these rims do not clear Cobra, Bullitt, or Mach 1 brakes. Changing the calipers to the GT brakes, or to an aftermarket drag caliper like the Aerospace brand, allows the narrow wheel to fit without interference.

Companies like Weld and Bogart build quality wheels designed for drag slicks and front runners. These lightweight aluminum wheels are specifically designed for drag racing, and can be ordered in custom offsets and designs to fit exactly as the customer desires. Although these wheels are very strong in the intended application, they are not designed for side loads, and should never be used on the street. If you want a lightweight drag-style wheel for your street Mustang, Weld does make a similar wheel designed for the street that's capable of withstanding the side loads incurred on the road.

Drag slicks can be of either tube or tubeless design, depending on the manufacturer. If they are a tube design, it's usually a good idea to screw the tire to the rim. A series of holes are drilled around the bead flange and short sheet-metal screws are installed, preventing the tire from spinning on the rim. Another approach is a bead lock wheel, where the bead of the tire is secured between an outer ring and the wheel itself. This is an effective solution that tends to be used on the larger Pro-Stock-style slicks on the 2,000-hp Mustangs running in Pro 5.0 classes.

The last item on our wheel agenda is wheel studs and nuts. The stock studs are fine, but the drag-racing sanctioning bodies require open-ended nuts with the stud extending through the nut, making it easy to visually confirm that a wheel nut has not backed off. On drag-oriented and road-race Mustangs, we like to use Moroso wheel studs.

The longer stud is made of premium grade steel, and has no threads on the end, which makes starting the nuts much easier. Premium wheel nuts should be installed at the same time. You need nuts with a tapered seat or mag style, depending on the wheel type. Wheel nuts should be torqued to 95 ft-lbs in a crisscross pattern with a torque wrench every time. This ensures

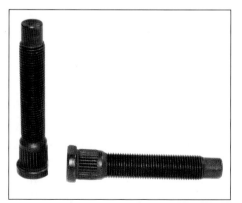

Racing wheel studs are manufactured from 8740 steel, are a full 4 inches long, and have a quick start end with no threads, ideal for pit stops.

Impact guns are fine for removing and installing wheels, but always final tighten the wheel nuts using a torque wrench, with the car on the ground, to a value of 95 ft-lbs.

This '03 Cobra features 3-piece polished DTM wheels. They're 18 x 9 inches in front, 18 x 10 inches in the rear, with 265/35/18 front tires and 285/35/18 rear tires, respectively.

the wheel does not loosen as the aluminum expands and contracts with temperature change.

Choosing Wheels

So, now you've decided on some tires, but you want to upgrade the wheels at the same time. There are a thousand different wheels available for Mustangs. How do you know which one is right for you? First thing you need to consider is diameter. Most of the time a 17- or 18-inch diameter wheel fulfills the requirements of a Mustang owner. Tire choices in those sizes are many, and they have enough sidewall height to provide some ride comfort and to protect the wheel from potholes. While 19- and 20-inch wheels look cool, they aren't terribly practical for day-to-day use. The skinny sidewall provides very little deflection, so they ride hard on the street, transmitting every small bump in the road directly into your body, and they are prone to damage from rough roads. Twenty-inch wheels certainly wouldn't last very long in Detroit, renowned for its car-sized

potholes. If you have a Mustang with 20s on it for car shows, it's probably realistic to have a second set for long distance cruising, saving your show rims for the show.

You may also have to choose a wheel that fits over a big front brake kit. Brembo, Wilwood, and StopTech brakes all require a 17-inch or larger wheel with a certain spoke shape and wheel offset in order to clear their calipers. Check with some experienced installers to see if your big brake kit works with a given set of wheels. Most mail order houses do not take wheels back if tires have been mounted on them, so this is important to know in advance. Wheel offset or backspace is a term used by the wheel industry to denote the location of the wheel mounting surface, in relation to the rim width. An eight-inch-wide wheel with zero offset would have four inches of the rim width on each side of the wheel mounting surface that butts up against the axle flange. A negative offset would move the mounting surface towards the inside edge of the rim, thereby moving the outer edge of the rim closer to the edge of

the fender. Conversely, a positive offset would move the rim closer to the centerline of the chassis. This relationship can also be expressed as backspacing, which refers to the distance between the wheel mounting surface and the back side of the rim in inches. So, an eight-inch rim with a five-inch backspace is the same thing as an eight-inch rim with one inch of positive offset.

In the case of the '94-2004 SN95 Mustang, a nine-inch-wide rim with a

Checking new wheels with a dial indicator before mounting your tires is always a good idea. The run out should not exceed .060 inch.

These BBS three-piece racing wheels are lightweight, strong, and available in a wide variety of offsets to suit any application. The individual sections of the wheels can be purchased separately, making it easy to replace a bent outer rim half.

six-inch backspace works pretty well. In 1999, the factory made the rear axle one inch wider, so the ideal offset may vary a bit for the later cars. In general, a 17 x 9 (front) and 17 x 10 (rear) or 18 x 9.5 and 18 x 10.5-inch combination works well on the Mustang. Many of people favor a wider wheel on the rear of the Mustang, along with a wider tire. I think it looks better, and a Mustang with 400 to 500 hp can certainly benefit from more rear tire than is feasible to carry inside the front fender. With the turning requirement of the front wheels, our tire size is limited in the front to about a 275 section tire. Even then, some scrubbing may occur during turning. A solution to scrubbing the tire or wheel against the anti-roll bar is to use a rack spacer that snaps in inside the steering rack bellows, limiting the travel of the steering rack. This allows the owner to customize the rack travel to suit his/her requirements. While this modification does reduce the turning circle slightly, it's usually so minimal that it's hardly noticeable, and it is cer-

tainly more pleasant than the sound of the wheel up against the anti-roll bar. On the rear, a 315-section tire can be fitted with the correct offset wheel and rolling of the outer fender lip.

Adding a wheel spacer is another option for fine-tuning the wheel and tire package. While not the ideal solution, spacers do provide a quick and cost-effective option for minor fitment issues. Spacers are available in thicknesses from 1/8 inch to 3/8 inch. I don't really recommend a spacer thicker than 5/16 inch on a Mustang, unless you add longer wheel studs too. We need to maintain at least 1/2 inch of thread engagement between the wheel stud and the wheel nut in order to securely connect the wheel and tire assembly to the axle.

When selecting an aftermarket wheel, what do we need to look for? Aside from the correct width and offset, we want a wheel that is relatively light, strong, and finished with a damage-resistant coating to stay looking good for a long time. Most one-piece wheels

are cast aluminum, machined after the casting process, and powder coated or epoxy painted to provide a tough, durable finish. All good-quality wheels have a sticker inside certifying that they meet SFI aftermarket standards, or a logo cast into the wheel itself that certifies that the wheel meets OEM standards. Even with quality wheels, a bad one occasionally slips through or gets

This wheel has adequate clearance between the upgraded caliper and the spoke. Measure before you buy, to avoid having to grind anything to get it to fit.

damaged during shipping, so I recommend checking new wheels for runout, prior to mounting tires on them. This is easily accomplished by bolting the wheel to the hub on the car and using a dial indicator mounted to a jack stand. The wheel should be round and concentric within .040 inches. Placing the dial indicator against the outer face of the rim checks for lateral run out, and placing the indicator on the bead-sealing surface inside the rim at 90 degrees to the face of the wheel checks for concentricity. Run out is the deviation from perfectly round on the OD of the wheel, or the variance from parallel between the hub mounting surface and the wheel face. If it's off by more than .040 inches, the wheel should be rejected. This is also a good procedure to follow with wheels used at open track events on a regular basis. Rims get bent from bouncing off curbs or at track events, and then we wonder why the car has developed strange handling attributes. Bent wheels make great hose reels and coffee tables.

If you have the budget for three-piece modular wheels, some lovely stuff is out there. BBS, Fikse, HRE, and others combine a cast or billet center with spun aluminum outer halves. One advantage to a three-piece wheel is the ability to get custom offsets that are not always readily available in one-piece wheels. Another plus is the reparability factor. If you bend a one-piece wheel it's usually not cost effective to repair it, but a three-piece wheel, can be restored to new with another outer rim half. The three-piece wheels are usually bolted together using high-tensile bolts, and servicing them should be left to the wheel manufacturer. Three-piece wheels are most commonly used for road racing where the reparability and reduced weight are advantages. These benefits are not justified on a street car, but the unique designs available in modular wheels may be reason enough for some who desire an exclusive look.

The Goodyear tire pressure monitoring system can be installed easily. The sensors, mounted inside the tire, supply up-to-the second information about the tire pressure via radio signal, alerting the driver in the event of pressure loss.

Balancing aftermarket wheels should always be done on a dynamic tire balance machine, which spins the wheel to measure the imbalance. It's possible to place all the balancing weights on the inside of the rim where it doesn't detract from the aesthetics of the wheel. Stick-on weights should always be used, and we add duct tape on top to prevent the weight from coming off if the adhesive fails. Cleaning the rim with a mild detergent and a Scotch-Brite pad provides a clean surface for the stick-on weight to adhere to. Adding more than three to four ounces of weight to balance a wheel and tire assembly is a sure sign of a problem with either the tire or the wheel, and deserves investigation.

I prefer to use metal valve stems on high-performance wheels. They are more durable than the stock rubber stems, and are required for competition use in drag racing classes and by some other sanctioning bodies. When filling the tires, we often use nitrogen if the car is to be used at the track. All compressed air has some water vapor in it, which expands with heat. Tire pressure increases in the tire as the temperature of the tire increases, but using nitrogen dramatically reduces the amount of change, producing a more consistent pressure and reducing potential corrosion inside the wheel.

The curved spoke of the ROH 17- x 9-inch wheel easily clears the Brembo brake upgrade on this Mustang GT. Wheel companies often do not know for certain if their wheels clear certain brake kits, so it's best to check with an installer who has had experience in fitting wheels to Mustangs with big-brake kits.

Monitoring your tire pressure is extremely important in some motorsport events like the Silver State Challenge, an open road race held in Nevada. A sudden loss of air pressure can cause catastrophic tire failure, resulting in fatal accidents. The tire companies don't even want to know about competitors using their tires in this activity because of the risk of tire failure due to excessive heat and sharp stone punctures. On-board tire monitoring systems have become required equipment at the top level of this competition. OEMs have been using tire pressure monitoring systems on sports cars without room to carry a full-size spare.

If your mini spare no longer fits because of mods, Goodyear has a nifty on-board tire pressure monitoring system. This system can be installed on your Mustang, providing a warning of an impending flat, in addition to continual pressure information without having to manually check the tires every time. A simple sensor is placed in each wheel, built into the tire valve. The information is displayed on the corner of a new rear view mirror supplied with the kit. For around $500, this system, and a can of tire inflate/sealer, allows you to ditch the mini spare. Pretty slick.

Suspension

Wheelie bars affect the launch, according to adjustment. The shoe polish on the wheels tells the crew how hard each wheel is hitting the track during launch, providing valuable feedback for suspension tuning.

Offset polyurethane steering-rack bushings raise the rack on its mounting bolts, offsetting some of the negative bumpsteer created when lowering springs are installed.

The Mustang suspension uses a lower front A-arm supported with a coil spring anchored to the K-member. A semi-McPherson strut links the spindle with the body shell and acts as a damper. At the rear, the solid axle is suspended on coil springs with long lower links and angled upper links to locate the axle laterally. The IRS used on the later-model Cobra's uses unequal length A-arms with coil springs mounted to a cast rear upright with locating links providing toe adjustment.

The major shortcomings on the front suspension are the friction in the front struts created during the cornering process. This can bind the front strut and limit the cornering forces that can be generated. On the rear, the angled upper links don't do a great job of laterally locating the axle. The IRS has design issues that create substantial wheel hop under standing start launches.

The first order of business in tuning the suspension system is to reduce bushing flex. Reducing the compliance of the OEM rubber bushings helps keep the suspension links from deflecting at the chassis attachment points under high acceleration, braking, and cornering loads. For street cars that see some weekend warrior duty at the race track or drag strip, urethane front control-arm, steering-rack, and rear control-arm bushings provide improved control with a harsher but still acceptable ride on the street. An additional benefit of replacing the front lower control-arm bushings with urethane bushings is that we can choose offset bushings, which move the lower

Offset urethane control-arm bushings reduce busing flex and increase front end caster at the same time.

These Steeda lightweight aluminum tubular control arms are for serious racers. Notice there is no place to hook up a rear sway bar.

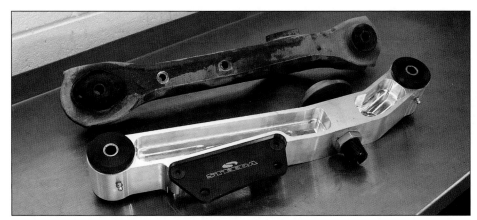

These CNC billet aluminum control arms have adjustable spring perches so you can raise or lower your rear end. This is especially handy when swapping on a different sized drag slick or corner-weighting your Stang. They're also much stronger than the factory arms.

control arm forward in the chassis for more caster. Increasing the front caster angle increases the negative camber on the front wheel during cornering, providing a higher level of grip.

I favor caster angles in the five to seven degree range, and the offset lower control-arm bushings are just one of the tools in our box of tricks to help us achieve this alignment setting. Some manufacturers offer bushings with two or more different types (hardnesses) of urethane. One level of hardness provides some ride comfort through road isolation, while a firmer material locates the suspension member more precisely. These dual-hardness bushings are a great solution for street-driven cars, where you don't want a harsh-riding car, but you do want improved suspension control and response.

In particular, changing the steering-rack bushings to urethane or even aluminum bushings has a dramatic effect on steering response. Instead of a nano-second delay between turning the steering wheel and getting a response at the front tires, you get instant response with the stiffer bushings. If your car has lowering springs, you should choose offset steering-rack bushings. Offset rack bushings move the rack up about 1/4 inch, realigning it with the steering arm. This restores the original geometry, reducing the bump steer in the front suspension.

Rear Control Arms

At the rear of the solid-axle Mustang, you can replace the upper and lower control-arm bushings with urethane. This is a really good idea if the car is four or five years old or has high mileage on it. OEM bushings deteriorate so slowly that often the driver doesn't really realize how sloppy the suspension has become. While replacing just the bushings is one option, and an economical one at that, you could just replace your upper and lower arms with aftermarket units that come with urethane bushings installed. Besides having new, stiffer bushings, boxed or tubular control arms resist bending and twisting more than the stock arms, and some offer additional adjustability. Several different types of aftermarket control arms are available, beginning with boxed steel arm, moving through

These Steeda lightweight aluminum tubular control arms are for serious racers. Notice there is no place to hook up a rear sway bar.

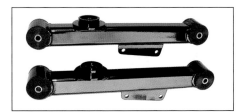

A type of lower control arm is available for every use and budget. These are Steeda's steel boxed control arms. They're affordable, stronger than stock, and come with polyurethane bushings on both ends.

tubular aluminum arms, and ending up with fully CNC-machined billet arms. All these types offer different benefits at different price points. The boxed steel arms are usually the least expensive, but they may in fact be heavier than the stock arm that they replace. The extra weight of a steel arm is not much of a detriment on a street car, but a road racer would prefer the lighter unsprung weight of an aluminum arm. Hotchkiss, Maximum Motorsport, Mr. Gasket, and other companies all sell steel control arms. The Mr. Gasket lower arm relocates the pickup points at the axle attachment point, creating additional mechanical advantage for the lower arm, planting the tire into the pavement under acceleration.

Steeda produces several types of rear lower control arms. Their lightweight aluminum tubular arms come with a

Adjustable upper control arms allow you to adjust your pinion angle. The right pinion angle can give you a better launch, more traction, or just keep away any unwanted vibrations.

These spherical upper-control-arm bushings replace the factory rubber bushings in your differential housing for solid axle location.

choice of busing types. This makes them a favorite for street/autocross/open-track cars, and street/strip drag cars. Their newest lower arm is a lightweight billet CNC lower control arm with an adjustable spring perch, allowing the owner to adjust ride height. I just love using that piece since it makes adjusting the ride height on the car such a breeze. These billet Steeda lower control arms are available with urethane bushings for street cars or solid heim joints for racecars.

Upper rear control arms are available in fixed and adjustable versions from several manufacturers. Adjustable-length upper control arms allow you to tune the pinion angle of the differential. Changing the pinion angle changes the amount of bite the car has at the dragstrip or coming off the corners of the road race circuit. Adjusting the pinion angle to between three and six degrees down at the front of the differential causes the normal torque reaction in the driveline under acceleration to plant the rear axle assembly hard towards the pavement, increasing the vertical load on the tire and improving traction. Setting the pinion angle is best done on a drive-on hoist. Unhooking the driveshaft from the differential lets you place an angle finder on the pinion flange, measuring the pinion angle. From there, increasing or decreasing the length of the upper links adjusts the pinion angle.

Dual-purpose cars or cars used primarily at the track should use adjustable upper control arms with a spherical bushing that transmits all of the force to the tire right away. Replacement bushings are also available for the upper bushing located on the top of the differential. These are available in both urethane and spherical. I like using the Steeda spherical end on all drag race, road race, and hard-core street cars. I also recommend a spherical bushing on the body end of the upper link for drag cars, but a urethane bushing for road race, open track, and street cars that need a little bit of give.

Cars that see extreme track use benefit from having plates welded in at the chassis attachment points for the upper and lower control arms. This prevents the bolt holes from becoming ovaled out through repeated use and stress. Mig-welding a mild steel plate with a drilled and reamed hole in the center is very little work for the added benefit and peace of mind. The angled upper control arms also locate the rear axle laterally, and reducing suspension bushing flex and slop around the mounting holes means locating the axle more firmly, reducing rear steer as the car rolls during cornering.

A quick note on installation techniques: Do not torque the fasteners on the front and rear control arms unless the car is resting on its wheels on a drive-on hoist. Tightening these fasteners in any other position preloads the bushings, adding additional suspension friction.

IRS

The IRS-equipped Cobra has its own requirements as far as upgrading the suspension bushings and links. First, we replace the stock rear subframe bushings that mount the subframe to the chassis with our own aluminum bushings. This is not a moving joint and very little increase in harshness results from doing this. Urethane versions of the subframe bushing are also available, too. Now that the subframe is properly located, replace the lower rear control-arm bushings with improved urethane bushings. Bushing deflection in the IRS cars creates more problems than in a solid axle car because it causes changes in toe angles. It can also cause the car to rear steer, have high-speed instability, and a host of other problems not seen in a solid axle car. Trail braking in particular, a technique where the driver is braking well into the first part of the corner, can cause the front bushing on the IRS control arm to deflect, causing the tires to toe-out during cornering. This is liable to cause the rear end of the car to step out suddenly, causing an uncomfortable moment for the driver.

Some aftermarket upper and lower arms available for the IRS are out there, but I have to say that our experiences with them to date have not been good. The arms that we used were manufactured from moly tubing, and we had some crack near the welds and fail. This

Solid press into the differential housing cage to solidly locate the axle. Stiffer bushings transmit more vibration into the body, but in many cases, it's worth it.

This IRS upright has heavy-duty spherical bearings installed to properly locate the suspension under high cornering loads. The OEM bearing is encased in a soft plastic material that deforms rather easily, allowing slop in the suspension.

These aluminum IRS differential bushings allow you to make pinion angle adjustments by adding or taking out shims.

is unacceptable. In at least one case, it could have caused a serious accident. My recommendation at present is to stick with the OEM arms with upgraded bushings. We have experience using the production arms since 1999, and I have to say, we have never had a failure with them. One thing we do recommend is replacing the OEM spherical joints in the rear uprights with a solid type. The stock spherical bushing is surrounded by a Teflon material that gets pounded out under load and creates slop in the rear suspension. Substantial machining is required to install the spherical bushings, but the results are worth the effort. This is a valuable modification for both road race and drag race type IRS cars, and it is suitable even for street driven cars.

I have one comment about spherical bearings in general. No matter where they're located in the suspension system, urethane and rubber bushings can be installed and basically forgotten about – not so with spherical ends. The spherical bearing is subject to wear from dirt contamination, water exposure, and they need to be checked, cleaned, and replaced on a regular basis. If this doesn't suit your idea of Mustang maintenance, stick with the urethane bushings and you'll be happier.

Continuing with IRS mods, the pinion bushings should be replaced with aluminum ones, and the pinion bushing bracket can be upgraded with a heavy-duty unit from Kenny Brown. The stock rubber pinion bushings deflect too much, and urethane bushings melt with the high temperatures developed in the aluminum IRS case, so aluminum is the way to go.

The aluminum pinion bushing kits contain shim washers, which allow us to optimize the pinion angle, just as with a

solid axle. Once again, for serious track duty, the IRS subframe can benefit from selective welding and some well-placed gussets to reduce flex in the system.

Bumpsteer

Okay, now that the suspension links are sorted, let's move on to some of the other components in the system. Steeda manufactures a dynamite X2 ball joint for the SN95 Mustang. The X2 ball joint raises the front roll center up. The roll

With the original ball joint on the left and the Steeda X2 ball joint on the right, it's easy to see how the X2 ball joint raises the spindle, relative to the control arm, raising the roll center on the front suspension.

center of a suspension system is the point about which the sprung mass of the vehicle rolls under cornering forces. Both the front and the rear suspension have their own roll center. With a higher front roll center, you can use softer front springs and anti-roll bars, which gives you better grip on rough surfaces. This is a worthwhile modification for any corner-carving Mustang.

When you lower your Mustang, you also create bumpsteer in the front-end steering geometry. Bumpsteer is the condition where the toe changes in or out when the suspension moves up and down, like say during cornering, braking, acceleration, or when you hit a

Adjusting the bumpsteer on the car consists of adding or subtracting the various shims at the outer tie rod end stud, and checking the toe change through the suspension travel, to obtain the minimum amount of toe change possible.

bump in the road. This is a very undesirable characteristic, as the suspension – not the driver – is steering the car. With a lowered Mustang, the lower control arms are no longer parallel to the tie rods, and while raising the rack with the offset bushings helps to place the tie rods parallel with the lower control arms again, it does not eliminate the bumpsteer problem. The solution is to add a bumpsteer kit to the front end along with the offset bushings.

Bumpsteer kits have a spherical rod end that replaces the stock outer tie-rod end and spacers that allow us to adjust the height of the rod end relative to the steering arm. The objective is to adjust the rod end to minimize the toe change throughout the suspension travel. We can plot the toe change and create a bumpsteer curve, and then plot our new curve to see the result of our changes.

In order to adjust the bumpsteer, we need to be able to move the suspension through its full range of motion. This is usually difficult with the springs installed, so it's best to remove them, support the car on a jack at the ride height, and measure the bumpsteer at one-inch increments in both the jounce and rebound conditions. A bumpsteer gauge can be readily constructed using a dial indicator and a piece of wood, or you can use an alignment machine if

one is available. Simply add or subtract spacers until you have the setup with the least bumpsteer.

Bumpsteer correction is important on drag cars as well as open-track/road-racecars. In the case of a drag car, the objective is to minimize the bumpsteer when the front suspension is in full droop, as this is where the suspension is when the car leaves the line with the front wheels dangling in the air. Limiting the suspension travel on the front end with stainless steel wire cable also limits the toe change by reducing the range of motion.

Caster/Camber Plates

Caster/camber plates allow you to adjust the alignment of your front suspension beyond what the factory originally planned for. Caster/camber plates are available from several manufacturers, each with their own design.

Adjustable caster/camber plates (above) provide easily adjustable front-end settings versus extremely limited range of adjustment on OEM strut mounts (below). The spherical bearing in the caster/camber plate eliminates the flex inherent in the stock rubber mount.

Caster/camber plates can be manufactured from both steel and aluminum, and either works effectively. The key thing to look for when sourcing caster/camber plates is the bearing and type of retention system used to secure the bearing in the plate. In order to move the top of the strut for alignment, the spherical bearing in the plate needs to be able to move laterally and operate at different angles. All the shock loads are transmitted through the bearing assembly, and if the bearing is of dubious quality, or if the fit of the bearing and retaining ring or collar are loose in the plate, movement occurs, and the bearing pounds out the bore of the plate in no time. Dirt or water contamination also creates accelerated bearing wear, resulting in steering binding and free play in the top shock mounting. Keep an eye on the spherical bearings and service as necessary. Both three- and four-bolt caster camber plates are available. The four-bolt plates provide less deflection under load, and therefore are the better choice for racing. Either is satisfactory for street use.

With all the adjustment now available with the addition of these aftermarket products, you need some alignment specifications to work with. Here are three different alignment recommendations, depending on the type of use. I am going to break this down into street, open-track, and race settings.

Street Alignment
The street adjustments offer optimum performance in real-world driving. For example, you are seldom going to get a tire near optimum temperature on the street, and if you can run hard enough to get the tires up to temp, the authorities will probably have you incarcerated. With this in mind, we don't need large camber angles, one degree being the maximum you should use on the street. Toe is kept at zero to help with turn in. Zero toe occasionally creates some tram lining, where your tires want

Alignment Specifications			
	Caster	Camber	Toe
Street	4-5°	-1°	0
Open Track	6-7°	-1.5° to -2-1/2	.125" out
Road Race	6-7°	-2° to -3-1/2	.125" out
Drag Race	6-7°	0°	0 to .125" in

Caster/camber plates can be made of steel or aluminum, with spherical bearings or rubber bushings at the tops of the struts. They allow you to adjust the caster and camber beyond factory settings for optimal performance handling.

to follow the depressions in the roads caused by all the traffic traveling in the same path. This characteristic is accentuated by wide tires, and is particularly troublesome in the slower lane favored by trucks. This is just another reason to keep the pedal down and use the left lane (like we needed a reason).

Open-Track Alignment

For a good open-track setup, add some negative camber (shoot for -1-1/2 to -2-1/2 degrees) on the front end to keep the tire contact patch near optimum as the cornering loads and speeds increase. At this stage, you're likely using R-compound tires or at the least stickier street rubber, and the increased speeds and cornering G's are going to heat the tire surface up to a level where the overall mechanical grip of the tire improves. Increasing the toe-out to 0.125 to 0.150 inch improves corner turn in by accentuating the Ackerman effect early in the corner entry phase. Ackerman is the built-in design geometry that causes a car's inside front tire to pivot more for a given steering input than the outside tire.

This compensates for the fact that the outside front tire follows a larger arc than the inside tire around any corner. While manufacturers build some Ackerman into most steering systems, improved turn-in can still be gained from increased toe-out. Although this toe-out increases drag on the inside front tire, in a competition situation the inside tire is much more lightly loaded while cornering. Thus, toe-out helps more than it hurts.

The goal of this open-track alignment is to enhance two main areas of cornering performance. The first is initial turn-in — in other words, the transition between driving on the straight and steady state cornering. Our objective is to have the car turn in readily, not slide out or feel nervous during this transition. The smoother the transition is from straight-ahead to steady-state cornering (where the car has entered the turn, rolled over on its suspension and taken a set), the more confident the driver is. During the middle part of the corner, our objective is for the car to maintain its steady-state cornering speed and respond to minor corrections in a predictable fashion, maintaining the desired

trajectory through the corner. Finally, the last phase of the corner is where the driver is applying power, and unwinding the steering wheel. This last phase of the corner is not as affected by changes in alignment as the first two.

The corner entry is the most important part of the corner, and unfortunately, it's usually complicated by the fact that we're hard on the brakes at the time. This means that the car is compressing the front suspension during turn-in. Keep this in mind when you're adjusting the bump-steer curve. The toe change under compression is going to affect turn-in more than the toe change while the suspension is extended in rebound mode. There are a few situations where we need to turn into a corner while the front tires are almost off the ground, but they are few and far between, and the ultimate speed those corners can be taken at has less to do with the alignment than with the skill and bravery of the driver.

Static toe-out on the road-race setup is going to be in the .200 to .250 inch range, and camber should be -2 to -3.5 degrees or so. The camber on a track car varies somewhat depending on the type of tire, tire pressure, the track, and driving style. The temperature of the tire taken across the tread using a pyrometer is useful in determining optimum camber settings. The objective is to get the tire surface temperature as even as possible across the tread. The alignment settings above are a suggestion, a starting point that can be fine-tuned to different tracks and driving styles as required. Quick lap times are achieved when the car is well set up to maximize cornering speed and the mechanical grip of the tire. However, successful racing requires a car that can be turned into a corner late, under heavy braking, as most passing opportunities occur under braking into a corner, particularly a slow corner. The car that can turn in later and out-brake his/her opponent wins the race into the corner, even if the ultimate cornering speed is slower than the other car. It is for this reason that I place a high degree of importance on the corner entry attributes. When you're adjusting a car for a particular track, always remember that two or three corners on any given track are important keys to success at a particular venue. Adjusting the car to favor those corners, while giving up a bit on some of the other less-important aspects, pays dividends.

Drag-Race Alignment

The objective on the drag alignment is to minimize tire scrub during all phases of track operation. A good drag race alignment has lots of caster – six or seven degrees – to help the car to go straight. Camber should be 0 to -1/4 degrees at ride height, as the car tends toward positive camber when the front end lifts. The front end of the drag car is seldom at actual ride height. Even at the top end of the track the car is pulling hard enough to create some upward motion on the front suspension. Toe-in should be 0 to .125 inch, and the bump-steer should be set to minimize toe change under acceleration.

Springs

The average Mustang enthusiast's first suspension modification is to install a set of lowering springs. The car sits too high as delivered from the factory, and too much gap is left between the tire and the fenderwell. The best factory springs produced were the ones used on the 2001 Bullitt. While these cars still sat a tad too high, the spring rates themselves were pretty good. They had decent handling and weren't too harsh over the bumps – the specially valved Tokico shocks and struts probably helped, too.

When you lower your Mustang, your goal should be to improve the look and the handling characteristics. But with so many choices on the market, which is best? First off, the ideal amount to lower an SN95 Mustang is 1-

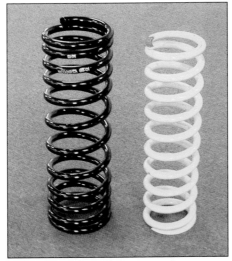

Here is a comparison between a progressive spring (on the left) and a linear spring (on the right). With a progressive spring, after the first two coils are compressed, there are fewer active coils, so the spring rate increases.

1/4 inches in the front, and 1 inch in the rear. Lowering the front end more than that creates suspension geometry issues that can result in poor handling. We don't want to lower the rear quite as much, because we want some rake. Having the rear 1/2 to 1 inch higher is usually good for an aggressive stance. With that out of the way, what sort of springs should we be looking for? Most of the available springs are progressive-rate springs. Some coils are wound closer together. As the suspension compresses, these coils contact each other all the spring rate increases.

Progressive springs may have an initial spring rate of, say, 400 lbs for the first inch of travel, and then rise to 550 lbs after the tighter wound coils are no longer active. This is nice on a street car because you get reasonable ride quality on the road, but when you really push the car, that higher secondary spring rate resists compression. Eibach, Steeda, and H&R are just a few companies with decent street spring kits. Spring rates for these springs are higher than stock, which reduces body roll and

sharpens steering response, but these spring kits are designed for street driving – not racing.

If you want to take a step up from the standard street spring kits for your open-track or road-racecar, check out a set of specific-rate springs. Specific-rate springs have a single spring rate, delivering predictable cornering. If you look at the spring rates on some of the competition springs, the spring rate number seems pretty high, but that isn't always the whole truth. You also need to consider the motion ratio. The motion ratio is the mechanical advantage of the suspension link relative to the spring and pivot placement. An SN95 Mustang has a front motion ratio of 0.5, which means an 800-lb front spring actually provides a wheel rate of 400 lbs. The wheel rate is the force required to move the wheel upwards. This means that for every 400 lbs added to one front corner, that corner lowers 1 inch. Since we are constantly transferring weight while cornering, the spring rate determines the amount of suspension travel during cornering. The motion ratio on the IRS rear suspension is also 0.5, and the solid axle is 1, as the spring acts directly on top of the axle. My recommendations for spring rates on open-track/road-race applications are: 850-900-lbs/in front; 180 lbs/in rear on a solid-axle car; and 700-750 lbs/in rear on an IRS car, depending on what anti-roll bars you use.

With the solid rear axle, we want the spring to be as soft as possible to aid in applying the power on corner exit. If you use a spring that's too stiff, wheel spin occurs. Conversely, the IRS rear suspension responds more favorably to stiffer rear springs and a lighter rear anti-roll bar, allowing the IRS left and right control arms to function independently of each other, improving traction on corner exit.

When installing new springs, check and replace the spring insulators. Eliminate the rubber spring pads on an open-track or road-racecar, as they just add compliance in the suspension system. On a street car, you need the insulators in place to prevent squeak, so replace yours with new rubber insulators or heavy-duty urethane replacements.

Drag Spring

Drag-racing Mustangs have different spring requirements than those expected to turn corners. The front spring on a drag car needs to have some stored energy to help transfer weight to the rear during the launch. Look for a spring that provides a wheel rate of about 300 lbs, and make sure the spring is long enough that the shocks can fully extend. On the rear, a soft rear spring of 140 lbs allows the rear suspension to move without unloading the tires. Eibach produces a drag launch kit with specific-rate springs and an air bag that can be inflated inside the right rear spring, allowing the driver to adjust for the torque reaction at the start line. Many drag racers eventually elect to install coil-over springs on the front of their Mustangs, reducing front-end weight at the same time.

Drive the car for 10 to 20 miles before you get an alignment after installing new springs. Springs take a set after they have load applied to them, and you want to make sure that has happened before you finalize your alignment settings.

Tubular Crossmembers, Coil-Overs, & Alternate Suspension Systems

I've kind of lumped all these subjects together because they are all interrelated. Tubular K-members are often used to reduce front-end weight. Most tubular K-members require you to use the manufacturer's own tubular lower A-arm and a coil-over spring conversion, since no provision for a stock-type spring is available. These can work okay for drag racing, but I am not a fan of these systems on street or track cars. Let me explain.

First, many of the aftermarket K-members and lower control-arm packages are made of lightweight moly tubing. This may be fine for drag racing, but

where the car does not receive many miles during a race weekend, and inspection occurs frequently. Moly tubing is more brittle than mild steel, requires more skill to weld properly, and must be normalized after welding or it cracks. I have a customer with a brand-name tubular K-member who open tracks the car regularly. Several times in the past three years, the fabricated lower front A-arms cracked in critical locations. The arms have been repaired on several occasions. If you really want a tubular K-member on a street car or road-racecar, please purchase a mild steel version. The weight savings of the moly tubing is not worth the effort. Eat a few less hamburgers instead.

The second problem with aftermarket K-members is the coil-over setup. Coil-over kits require a bearing plate between the top spring cup and the underside of the camber/caster plate. They usually come with a Torrington roller bearing thrust washer, which can quickly become contaminated by water and dirt. At this point, the bearing begins to self-destruct, or merely creates additional friction in the steering system. Finally, the coil-over spring does not carry the suspension load through

the ball joint center, and as a result, creates stiction with the shock absorber due to the side loads throughout the range of suspension motion. If you are interested in getting a tubular K-member, several reputable manufacturers out there like Kenny Brown and Maximum Motorsport can put together a quality setup for you.

Alternative rear suspension systems are available too, all trying to improve on the factory design. Some utilize a torque-arm design, similar to the Camaro/Firebird; others relocate suspension links and all sorts of things. The problem with mixing and matching all these different systems is that you end up with a car that doesn't work properly because someone has changed the anti-dive or the roll centers, and the average owner doesn't have the time or expertise to sort it all out. Stick with the basics – springs, anti-roll bars, bushings, and buy the best dampers you can afford. You won't be sorry.

Anti-Roll Bars

An anti-roll bar is just a spring by another name. The only difference is that an anti-roll bar doesn't work all the time like a regular suspension spring, it

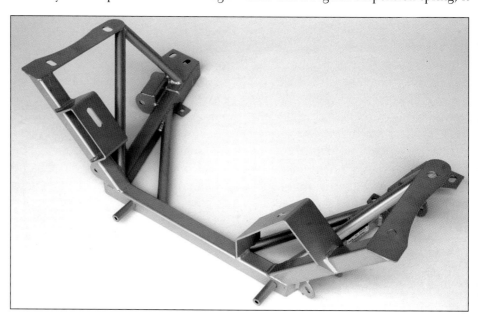

Tubular K-members like this one from Kenny Brown can save you a few pounds on the front end.

only works when the car is cornering. Anti-roll bars serve two functions on a performance car. First, they allow you to use lower-rate springs because they increase roll stiffness when the car is cornering. A lower-rate spring should conform more to the road surface and not skip over the bumps like a stiffer spring, allowing the tire to maintain the contact patch.

Second, anti-roll bars also give us a way to change the front/rear balance of the car. Road-racecars that race at many different tracks need a quick way to balance the handling from track to track. Changing springs is too time consuming and most series have limited amounts of practice time during a race weekend. Not to mention, if the weather changes at the last minute, say a torrential downpour starts 15 minutes before race time, the only practical way to adjust your suspension setup is with an adjustable anti-roll bars.

It's important not to get too hung up on the individual parts, but to make sure to have a system that works at the end of the day. The anti-roll bars supplement the springs on the car, keeping the car from rolling over on the edge of the tire. We need to have adequate overall spring rate (combination of suspension springs and anti-roll bars) to keep this from occurring. Beyond that, we can use anti-roll bars to balance the chassis through various types

of corners. Changing the anti-roll bar rate is similar to changing the spring rate at one end of the car. Increasing the front anti-roll bar rate (making it stiffer) increases the understeer (or push), while increasing the rear anti-roll bar rate increases the oversteer (or makes the car loose on the back end). Formula cars have anti-roll bars that can be adjusted by the drivers during the race from inside the cockpit. This allows the driver to adjust the car's handling as the tires wear, the fuel load changes, and track conditions change. While this is a bit over-the-top for the average Mustang, it illustrates how effective an anti-roll bar can be.

A simple way to increase the effective anti-roll bar rate is to substitute urethane bushings for the original rubber ones. The rubber bushings deflect in the brackets, making the bar less effective. The same thing is true with the brackets themselves, which are just steel straps. These straps flex under cornering loads, reducing the effective anti-roll bar rate. Steeda has some billet aluminum replacement brackets that reduce the flex.

Moving outboard, the anti-roll bar links used on the '96-2004 Mustangs already use urethane bushings from the factory. However, these can be worn after a few years and need to be replaced. The '94-'95 Mustangs did not come from the factory with urethane link bushings, so a new link kit with polyurethane bushings is recommended.

SN95 Mustangs came with front anti-roll bars that ranged in diameter from 25 to 30 mm. The larger the diameter of the anti-roll bar, the higher the effective spring rate. Generally, we like to replace the stock bar with a 35-mm front bar from Steeda. Addco also makes a 32- and a 35-mm front bar. Increasing the front anti-roll bar rate is going to reduce body roll and give more stability in corners. Unfortunately, increasing the front anti-roll bar rate also induces more understeer (or push).

Aftermarket front anti-roll bars are not usually adjustable, but some of the race-only bars certainly are. Multimatic Motorsport has a moly front anti-roll bar that they use on their Mustang racecars. It has four different end-link mounting holes that allow rapid adjustment at the track.

On the rear, the SN95 Mustangs came with 17-23-mm rear bar, depending on the model. Addco has 19-, 22-, and 25-mm rear bars available. Steeda has an adjustable rear anti-roll bar that can be adjusted quickly, altering the front-to-rear balance of the car. This is a good compromise for most performance Mustangs in conjunction with a larger front bar, since it gives you options. The factory anti-roll bar rates are designed to produce understeer, because understeer or push is the safest handling trait for the average driver. When the car begins plowing straight ahead in a corner, the natural

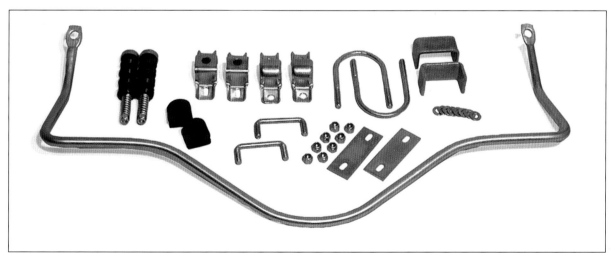

The Steeda adjustable rear anti-roll bar allows the driver to easily and quickly adjust the bar to suit different tracks or conditions.

If you open-track your car, you might want to set your front suspension up like this. This custom three-position adjustable front anti-roll bar allows you to quickly change the front roll stiffness from track to track.

response is to lift off the accelerator, scrubbing off speed. Performance drivers usually want less understeer, allowing the car to rotate while turning into corners. Since we want to keep the rear spring rate as soft as possible, especially on the solid-axle cars, a higher-rate rear bar assists in getting the car to rotate without increasing the rear spring rate excessively.

Should you be fortunate enough to race in the rain, tires do not generate anywhere near as much grip on a wet track as in the dry. This means that the car is not going to roll as much, and the roll stiffness and overall spring rates of the suspension are too high. Softening the anti-roll bars is a much easier and quicker method of adjusting the roll stiffness than changing springs. In fact, if it's really wet, disconnecting the end link on one end of the anti-roll bar quickly disables the bar. The car may well be faster and easier to drive with the bars disconnected. The overall balance of the car is much more important

in the rain as well. For a car that understeers or oversteers in the dry, these characteristics are even more pronounced in the rain.

Drag-Race Anti-Roll Bars

Drag race Mustangs use anti-roll bars in an entirely different way. Since the car is only going straight during a drag race, no cornering loads are acting on the anti-roll bars. Drag cars do not use a front anti-roll bar at all, and even a weekend warrior can disconnect the end links on the front anti-roll bar for a gain. The stock front anti-roll bar slows down the rate of weight transfer from the front to the rear, so unhooking it allows the front end to lift more quickly.

In the rear, replacing the OEM rear anti-roll bar with an aftermarket drag-race specific bar allows you to tune the launch characteristics. A chrome moly anti-roll bar, like the TRZ rear bar, is mounted between the chassis rails at the rear. It rides on roller bearings for low

friction. Threaded heim ends on the end links allow us to adjust the length of the links independently.

By preloading the right side of the anti-roll bar, the torque reaction, which occurs during launch, is unable to unload the left rear tire. The energy that would normally twist the chassis is converted into forward motion, improving the 60-ft time, and lowering the ET. This also provides a quick adjustment to compensate for varying levels of grip at the starting line from track to track. A competition rear anti-roll bar kit is recommended for any Mustang running 11s or quicker. It can be easily disconnected when you're not on the track. However, the stock tailpipes cannot be used with this type of rear anti-roll bar, as there is not enough clearance. TRZ and Steeda each make a nice competition rear anti-roll bar.

Shocks and Struts

Without dampers (shocks and struts), you couldn't drive your Mustang much above a walking pace. If you have ever driven a car with a broken shock, you know what I'm talking about. A damper's job is to dampen the oscillations of the spring during load transfer and over bumps. In other words, it resists the suspension's up-and-down motion. It does this by converting the kinetic energy in the spring into heat energy in the damper, and then dissipating the heat into the airstream.

This sounds easy enough, but it's a tough job. Dampers are velocity sensitive; that is to say, more damping occurs the faster the piston moves (as more vertical acceleration occurs). By modifying internal spring-loaded valves and metering orifices, you can tailor the damping characteristics to the specific requirements of a given car. Since dampers also influence the rate at which load is transferred, performance dampers have damping curves tailored to produce good transient characteristics, helping the car to take a set

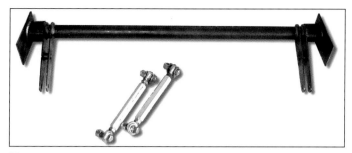

You can get an adjustable rear anti-roll bar for drag racing. Adjusting the end links preloads the chassis for a better launch.

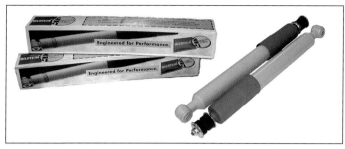

The Bilstein damper was OEM on the '03-'04 Cobra, and provides good damping with a comfortable ride. Bilstein also has aftermarket dampers for other versions of the SN95 Mustang.

quickly while cornering. You can purchase non-adjustable dampers, where the damping curve is preset by the manufacturer. You can also purchase a single-adjustable damper, which is adjustable in rebound (extension) only, or a double-adjustable damper, where both rebound and bump (compression) are user adjustable. Bilstein and Tokico Shocks are two examples of non-adjustable dampers. KYB Gas Adjust and Tokico Illumina dampers are examples of single adjustable dampers.

Koni makes both single- and double-adjustable shocks and struts. At the high end, Moton produces the double adjustable, remote reservoir Clubsport, designed for racers and open-track aficionados. A street car with the typical street suspension modifications really works nicely with a Bilstein, KYB, or Tokico. I like to use the Koni single adjustable dampers on dual-purpose street/strip or street/open-track cars, as the adjustable rebound damping allows the owner to drive daily in relative comfort, and adjust the dampers firmer for track work on the weekends.

Solid-axle cars like the SN95 Mustangs typically have a difficult time controlling the rear axle under hard braking and putting the power down on rough surfaces. Really good dampers like the Moton Club Sport series, with seven separate adjustments for both bump and rebound, allow the driver to adjust the damper characteristics to suit the track and the driving style. I recently did a test in a Mustang open-track car where we

compared the Moton Club Sport to Koni single adjustable dampers, and the difference was quite noticeable.

With the Konis, the solid rear axle would display axle tramp under hard braking. Adjusting the rebound valving in the Moton dampers eliminated the tramp. Increasing the rebound damping on the front Moton units allowed me to brake deeper into the corner, and the adjustable bump-valving made the car less unsettled driving over the curbing on corner exit. All in all, we were able to pick up a substantial amount of time on the circuit and improve the driver feedback from the suspension with simple damper adjustments. Although not inexpensive, a set of Moton Club Sport dampers are certainly worth the investment for a serious club racer or open-track driver.

Drag-race specific dampers such as the Koni SPA1 series, Lakewood drag shocks, and Strange Engineering dampers are designed differently from dampers used on the street or at road course. Each end of the car has specific requirements to maximize launch energy and produce a low ET. The Koni front dampers offer minimum resistance in rebound, thereby releasing the stored energy in the front springs during launch. Once the car has launched, compression damping on the front damper needs to allow the nose to settle as rapidly as possible, minimizing aerodynamic drag down the track. These Konis have five rebound positions, allowing you to tune the damper response to specific track conditions.

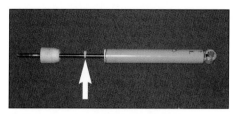

A tie wrap, installed around the damper shaft, can indicate the amount of suspension travel a car is experiencing at each corner.

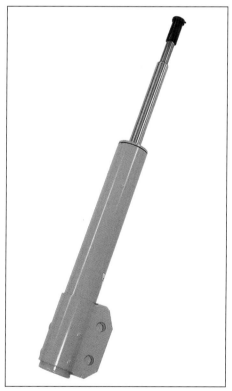

The Koni single adjustable damper has 2-1/2 turns of rebound adjustment available externally at the top of the damper. This allows the driver to rapidly adjust the dampers between street and track use.

The Koni rear dampers on a drag car have very little bump damping, and the rebound damping is digressive, which means they blow off at high piston speed. This keeps them from over-damping the rear during the launch and losing traction. The Lakewood dampers are not adjustable like the Konis, but they are an economical alternative, and they come in a 90/10 or a 70/30 valving for the front struts, and 50/50 for the rear dampers. A 90/10 strut has very little resistance in rebound to allow the car to lift the front end and transfer weight, and a lot of resistance to bump travel when the front end is settling after launch.

Strange Engineering Mustang struts and shocks come in somewhere between the Lakewood and the Koni on the price/value curve, offering 10-position external adjustment both front and rear. These Strange dampers are a great choice for dual-purpose street/strip car.

Rack and Pinions/ Steering Shaft Kits

The last items to touch in this chapter are rack-and-pinion units. While the standard Mustang power rack is suitable for just about every type of activity, some drag racers prefer to change over to a manual rack for the weight savings.

Flaming River makes a great manual replacement rack that bolts right into the SN95 chassis. On 1996 and later

These are Lakewood 90/10 front struts for the SN-95 Mustang. A strut with less rebound up front should help with weight transfer at the drag strip.

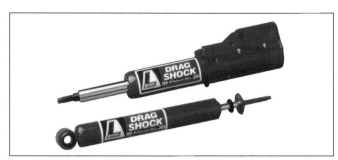

cars, eliminating the power rack and power steering pump also negates the hydro boost for the power brakes, so you need a manual master cylinder.

Flaming river also makes a heavy-duty steering shaft kit. We use these often on street, drag, and open-track cars. The needle bearing U-joints eliminate play in the stock shaft assembly, and the shaft kit retains the collapsible shaft design for safety during a crash.

Aftermarket shaft assemblies provide additional clearance for headers, improved resistance to exhaust temperatures, and they are available for both manual and power rack applications. Be sure to use thread locker on the set screws and jam nuts when installing the steering shaft assemblies. Without thread locking compound, we have found that these set screws loosen with time.

These Strange Engineering 10-position adjustable drag racing dampers are great for fine-tuning your setup for specific track conditions or different combinations of parts.

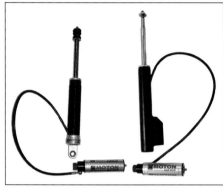

Moton Club Sport double-adjustable dampers have seven-position adjustment for both rebound and compression damping. The remote reservoir contains the nitrogen charge and the compression adjustment.

A manual steering rack conversion, like this one from Flaming River, saves considerable weight on a drag car when you factor in the power steering pump, hydroboost, and other items that can be eliminated.

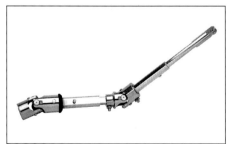

A heavy-duty steering shaft should be used on any track car. The OEM shaft has plastic components that can deteriorate in close proximity to the heat from long-tube headers.

Brakes

Along with all the upgrades to the rest of the Mustang for the 1994 model year, the brakes were also improved. Four-wheel disc brakes were now standard on every model – rear drum brakes were gone. ABS also became optional on all Mustangs beginning in '94. PBR two-piston front calipers, similar to the ones used by GM on the F-bodies and Covettes were introduced on the Cobra, along with larger 13-inch front discs.

All of this made a great improvement to a car that already had plenty of acceleration, but lacked in the braking department when compared with the Camaro/Firebird of the day.

Things only improved with the 2000 Cobra R, which came with four-piston Brembo front brakes, and even carbon-fiber brake ducts, standard from the factory. That's wonderful stuff, but for those of us without an R model, where should we begin to improve our brakes?

These glowing front rotors are a testament to how much heat is generated during braking. Street circuits like Trois Rivieres are particularly hard on brakes, with very little time between corners and no air movement on the course itself.

Brake Fluid

The easiest brake improvement is also the least expensive. Changing your brake fluid every 24 months on an every-day street car enhances braking perform-ance. Brake fluid is hygroscopic, which means that it has an affinity for water. A typical DOT 3 brake fluid, found in most cars, begins life with a boiling point around 400 degrees F. After only 24 months, water absorbed into the brake fluid can lower the boiling point over 100 degrees! The brakes are susceptible to fade as the fluid boils in the caliper, especially if the brakes are used two or three times in short succession.

The moisture absorbed into the brake fluid also causes premature corro-sion in the brake system, leading to ear-ly replacement of master cylinders and calipers. Some lube shops and garages are now testing brake fluid with elec-tronic testers to determine the amount of water absorbed and the actual boiling point of the fluid in some cases. While this is all well and good, I prefer to just change fluid based on time and usage. Consider brake fluid to be like some of the food in your refrigerator, you know, the stuff with a "best before" date on it.

The "best before" date on your brake fluid is 24 months from the date you drove your new car off the dealer's lot. If your Mustang is second hand, don't even think about it – just change it. Since this usually requires two people, just consider it a bonding opportunity with that special someone in your life. Obviously, if you use your Mustang for open track events like SVTOA events, or weekend drag racing, changing your brake fluid should become a more fre-quent event. Open-track driving demands that brake fluid be changed a week or two before the event, and bled after the event as well.

Weekend drag racers should change fluid at the beginning of every season, and then bleed the brakes once a week to once a month depending on speeds achieved and number of passes per weekend. Road racers already know all about brake fluid; that's why you see them bleeding the brakes virtually every time the car comes off the track, between practice, qualifying, and race sessions. Even the best fluid available can have localized boiling in some areas, and if you need a consistent, hard brake pedal, constant bleeding is required.

Different types of driving require different types of brake fluid. DOT 3 brake fluid is what your Mustang came with from Ford and the type most garages use to top up or change fluid. A typical DOT 3 brake fluid has a dry boiling point of 400 degrees F. The minimum level of brake fluid I recom-mend is DOT 4 fluid. A quality DOT 4 brake fluid has a dry boiling point of 500 degrees F, and is readily available at auto parts stores and even Wal-Mart. Castrol LMA and Valvoline Synpower are two commonly available brands. DOT 4 fluid is fine for every day cars, weekend drag racers, and the once-a-year open-track driver. Pro drag racers and open-track warriors (you know who you are), you guys and gals need some-thing better. Motul 600F is my pre-ferred fluid for this middle level of performance. It has a 600-degree-F dry boiling point, and it's reasonably priced at around $18 a pint. You need to find a performance outlet or mail order sup-ply house for performance brake fluid, as you are not likely to find it at the average auto parts store. Other good brands in this range are Wilwood Hi-Temp 570 F brake fluid and AP Racing 550 F brake fluid.

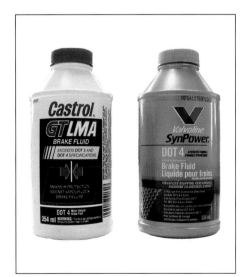

DOT 4 Brake Fluid is a good choice for a street-driven Mustang. Castrol CMA and Valvoline Synpower are two commonly available brands.

For open track and road racing, you want a brake fluid that can stand up to some heat. This Motul Racing brake fluid has a 600 degrees F dry boiling point.

This Tilton brake bleeding kit contains two bleeder bottles with hoses to attach to the brake bleeder nipples.

Brake bleeding is usually a two-person job: one in the car, and one outside to loosen and tighten the bleeder screw.

Solo-bleed screws allow one person to bleed the brakes by themselves. A spring-loaded check valve releases the fluid from the brake system and then reseals, preventing air from entering the brake system.

Professional road racers use Castrol SRF brake fluid. It costs $70 a quart, which is a lot of money by anyone's standards. But as with most things in life, you get what you pay for, and it's the best racing brake fluid available, period. It has a higher boiling point, at 660 degrees F, and works the best of any fluid in an extreme racing environment.

People ask, "What about DOT 5 silicone brake fluid, isn't it better?" The answer is yes, and no. DOT 5 fluid does not absorb water like a conventional fluid. Unfortunately, it also has a relatively low boiling point, which renders it useless for performance enthusiasts. It's also incompatible with other types of brake fluid, requiring a complete system flush. The best application for DOT 5 is for museum cars, which are seldom driven, and then only at moderate speeds.

So, now we know which type of fluid is appropriate for our needs, and next we need some equipment to help us bleed the brakes properly. A brake-bleeding bottle is nothing more than a clear container with a piece of transparent hose that slips over the brake-bleeding

nipple on the caliper. Tilton makes a dandy brake bleeding kit with two bottles and hoses, or you can make your own for next to nothing. Just take an old Gatorade bottle, cut a hole in the top, and get some clear nylon tubing from the hardware store. Just check that the plastic used to make the bottle won't dissolve when exposed to brake fluid by pouring a tiny bit of brake fluid in the container. Place the end of the tube over the bleeder nipple and the old brake fluid collects in the bottle. The clear tubing allows us to see when the old dark fluid is gone, and the new fluid has reached the bleeder. In a road-race car, watch the tubing for bubbles in the fluid, which is a sign of boiling fluid. Once all the bubbles have disappeared in the fluid traveling through the line, the boiled fluid has passed.

Brake bleeding is best accomplished with the assistance of another person. One person sits in the car and operates the brake pedal, while the second person operates the bleeder screw. Make sure the master cylinder reservoir is full, and then pump the brake pedal three or four

times and hold. The person at the caliper then opens the bleeder screw, allowing the old fluid to travel out through the clear line into the bottle. Once the pedal has reached the floor, the bleeder screw is tightened. This process is repeated several times at each corner, filling the reservoir as required, until new fluid has reached each corner of the car.

Do not allow the master cylinder reservoir to get completely empty (keep filling it with new fluid). Air gets sucked into the lines, requiring you to start the process all over again. The brakes should be bled in the following sequence: right rear, left rear, right front, and left front (from the furthest away from the master cylinder to nearest). If you don't have anyone to help you do this, another option is to install solo bleeders. These are replacement caliper bleed screws with a built-in check valve. This allows one person to bleed the brakes by themselves, the only disadvantage being that you cannot see the quality of the expelled fluid when doing this by yourself.

Brake Lines

Replacing the stock flex lines is another inexpensive brake upgrade. The original rubber flex lines expand slightly under the enormous brake pressure (1000 psi) exerted while braking hard. Braided stainless flex lines are available from aftermarket manufacturers such as Goodridge, Earl's, and Russell. These lines feature a Teflon inner liner combined with an abrasion-resistant stainless braided outer sheath. The Teflon does not expand under pressure like the original rubber line, creating a firmer, more consistent brake pedal.

Pre-made stainless flex lines are available for all SN95 Mustang front flex lines and some rear flex lines. With quite a few versions of rear flex lines in the various years and models, not all rear applications are available. In the event you need rear flex lines and none exist, fear not, for bulk line and fittings can be purchased, and custom lines fabricated. This is not a job for an inexperienced person. If you have not done this before, take your car to an experienced race shop and have them do it for you.

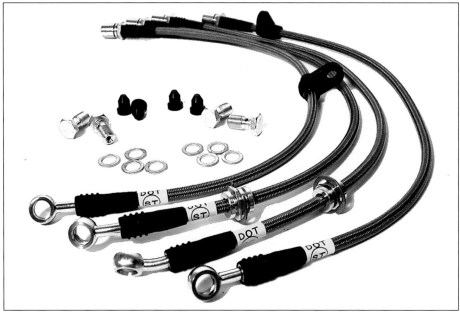

Braided stainless flex lines resist expanding under pressure, improving brake pedal feel.

Brake Pads

Changing the brake-pad compound on your Mustang can dramatically change its braking characteristics. Your original brake-pad compound was formulated to provide several different attributes. The pad material obviously had to stop the car, but additionally, the car manufacturer did not want brake squeal, or too much brake dust, which makes the wheels look nasty. The original brake pads also needed to be durable, lasting in excess of 60,000 miles for an average driver. Changing the brake pads to a performance-oriented compound improves certain aspects of braking performance, but you give some things up as well. A performance brake pad exhibits improved fade resistance and offers a higher coefficient of friction, resulting in shorter stopping distances. However, a high-performance street pad generally creates more brake dust than a standard pad, and a street/track brake pad often squeals when used on the street. Don't say I didn't warn you!

One thing seldom talked about when discussing brake upgrades is the fact that an upgraded brake system doesn't do much good if we exceed the capability of the tires. Once the brakes have locked the tire up, the car is not going to slow down any quicker. The amount of brake force that can be applied to any given tire is directly proportional to the amount of grip available to the tire. A performance tire that has a larger contact patch with the road surface and is manufactured with a stickier compound can absorb a higher braking force without losing grip with the road surface. So don't put a super-duper brake upgrade on your Mustang with the stock all-season tires and expect it to perform much better. If your tires are the limiting factor, upgrade them first.

In general, Cobras came from the factory with pretty decent brakes. Even with a tire upgrade, the brakes are up to the task for most track events. The '94-'98 V-6 and GT Mustangs on the other hand, do not have a surplus in the braking department. One hard stop from 100 mph is about all their braking systems can handle. The '99-2004 GTs were endowed with a larger-diameter rotor and an improved caliper design, which was a great improvement.

The 2003-'04 Cobra also came with underpowered brakes. We have a number of clients who open-track the late-model supercharged Cobra, and the stock brake pads are only good for three or four laps at a fast track like Mosport or Watkins Glen before pad fade sets in. Part of this is due to the fact that the cars are fairly fast right from the factory, and thus the entry speeds into the corners are quite high. They also have a lot of weight on the front end of the car and have minimal airflow to cool the brakes. Again, changing to a brake pad with a more aggressive compound is a good start.

Hawk Performance makes a line of brake pads with an assortment of compounds designed to cover a wide array of applications. Hawk HP Street pads are great for the Mustang enthusiast who wants a better-quality brake pad than the

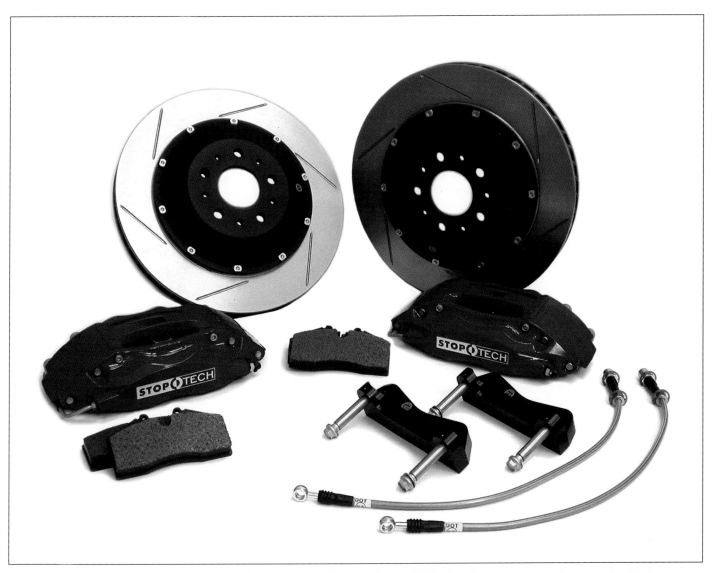

StopTech brake upgrade kits include 4-piston brake calipers, slotted 13-inch rotors, aluminum brake hats, high-performance brake pads, and stainless brake lines. (Photo courtesy StopTech)

original, that doesn't create brake squeal, and is good for the occasional autocross or open-track event. The HP Plus brake pad is a dual-purpose brake pad for the enthusiast who drives the car on the street, but needs a brake pad to use at open-track events with superior performance and fade resistance. Hawk also has several motorsport compounds to choose from as well. Motorsport compound brake pads should never be used on the street. A true-race compound brake pad requires several brake applications to get the pad compound hot enough to actually work properly. This is not what you want on the street. You

need a brake pad that works immediately at peak performance – even cold. Satisfied Brakes produces another excellent range of brake pads. They offer their Gransport range of brake pads, which encompass everything from performance street to endurance race compounds. Satisfied Gransport brake pads come standard with StopTech brake upgrades.

If you install a new set of performance brake pads in your Mustang, don't forget to bed the pads in. During the manufacturing process, the brake pad material has binders added, which hold the solid particles together until the

brake pads are completed. These binders contain oils that evaporate when the brake pads are used initially. When these oils come to the surface, a condition known as green fade occurs. Green fade, unlike regular pad fade, occurs only during break-in and does not occur again. However, if the pads are not allowed to cool down to ambient temperature after green fade occurs, they will never perform properly.

The correct way to bed pads in is to drive the car at a 50 to 60 mph speed and brake down to about 10 mph several times in succession. After doing this six to ten times, the brakes

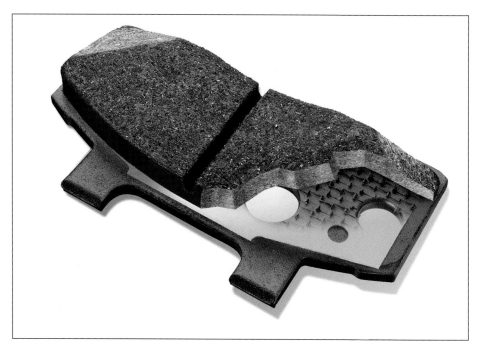

This cutaway drawing of a Satisfied Gransport brake pad illustrates the backing plate, pad material bonded to the plate, and the thermal barrier, which reduces the amount of heat transferred into the brake caliper. (Photo courtesy Satisfied)

begin to fade somewhat. This is the green fade, and the car should be parked and allowed to cool down for at least an hour. All performance brake pads, whether street or race compound, should be broken in the same way. Some manufacturers such as Performance Friction offer racing brake pads that have been broken in on a brake dynamometer, saving the race teams the time and expense of bedding in brake pads for races. This is also useful during times when it rains all weekend at the track, because you can't break in pads when it's wet outside. One note here about mixing and matching brake compounds: sometimes we can optimize the overall braking in a Mustang by using different compounds on the front and rear calipers. Just remember that the front brakes do 75 percent of the work, and we don't want the rear brakes to start slowing the car sooner or have a higher brake torque than the fronts, so use the more aggressive compound up front.

Brake Rotors

The more aggressive your brake pads are, the quicker the rotors are going to wear. Cast iron is used in brake rotors because it is cheap, long-wearing, remains ductile, and is not prone to cracking through numerous heat cycles. The brake rotor design affects the performance of the brakes, particularly how effectively the rotor transmits the heat generated through braking. Air is drawn in through the center of the disc and expelled through the rotor vanes at the edge of the rotor. The more effective the rotor vane design is at transferring heat to the air passing through the vane, the better the overall brake performance is. The Mustang Cobra switched to Brembo-supplied rotors in 2001, and they are the best original-equipment rotor available on the Mustang (except the R models). Aftermarket replacement rotors tend to be built to a price point, so if performance is the objective, Brembo aftermarket rotors may be your best bet.

The cross-drilled and/or slotted rotors now popular in the aftermarket certainly look cool, but do they work? Yes, they do offer some performance benefit, mainly through offering a channel for worn pad material to escape. During heavy braking, a fire band exists between the brake pad and the rotor surface. As tremendous heat is generated, debris from the brake pad is sheared off and mixes with gasses formed in the semi-molten area between the rotor and the pad. The cross drilled holes or slots in the rotor face form an avenue for the gasses and debris to escape. With no way to escape, this excess material would get trapped between the rotor and the pad, glazing the surface and creating a less-effective brake condition. Cross drilling looks sexy, but slotted rotors perform just as well, wiping the entire surface of the pad every time it passes, and they're not prone to cracking like cross-drilled rotors. If you want track performance without having to replace rotors all the time, go for the slots. If you want the sexy look on the street, cross drilling is the way to go.

Cryogenically treated brake rotors are becoming more popular with the open-track and road-racing set in the last few years. Taking the rotors down to 300 degrees F below zero and slowly bringing them back up to ambient temperature changes the molecular structure of cast iron and steel, imparting a toughness to it that improves the wear characteristics.

Cryo-treating was first used in the machine tool industry, as high-speed CNC mills were tearing up tool bits at an alarming rate. Cryo-treated brake rotors are known to last two or three times as long as standard rotors. The small additional cost is more than offset by the savings for open track and road-race users.

Heat's impact on calipers is less appreciated. Although aftermarket race calipers generally withstand several

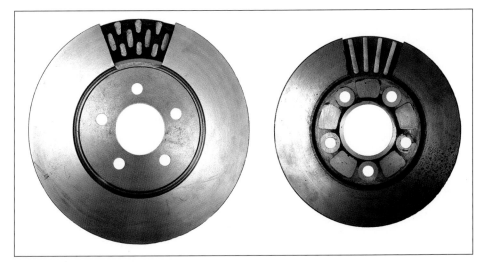

Here's a Cobra 13-inch rotor on left and a GT 11.65 inch rotor on right. They are partially cut away to show the different vane designs for cooling.

This StopTech rotor cutaway shows the directional vanes, designed to maximize heat dissipation. These aftermarket rotors are more thermally efficient than the OEM rotor. (Photo courtesy StopTech)

Finite element analysis software allows brake engineers to see the stress in the caliper during braking during the design process. The stiffer the caliper, the more consistent the braking.

races without servicing, the production Cobra calipers, when used by top teams in three-hour endurance races, were pitched in the dumpster every weekend along with the rotors. The incredible heat actually annealed the calipers, destroying the heat treatment of the original aluminum casting. Once soft, the caliper was prone to flexing, and the effectiveness of the brake system was compromised.

Calipers and Rotors

Fortunately for the Mustang enthusiast, several good off-the-shelf brake systems for any SN95 car are available. Probably the easiest place to begin is the Cobra-based upgrade for the '94-2004 Mustang GT. Ford Racing offers a front kit and a rear kit, both including production Cobra parts, allowing the owner to upgrade the front to 13-inch rotors, along with Cobra calipers and pads. The rear kit includes the 11.65-inch vented rotors, calipers, and all relevant hardware. These are very cost-effective upgrades for GT owners. It should be noted that the 2001 Mustang Bullitt and the 2003-'04 Mach 1 came with Cobra brakes, albeit with red painted calipers. The red calipers are also available through Ford Racing, for those who are so inclined. Upgrading the GT to Cobra calipers does require you to use 17-inch wheels for clearance.

Brembo produced a special four-piston caliper for the 2000 Cobra R that bolts directly to the SN95 spindle without adapters. This racing brake system includes slotted Brembo rotors, competition style pads, and stainless flex lines. It's available today through Ford Racing for a bit over $1,100 complete. For the money, this is an excellent brake upgrade for the Mustang, easily the best value for money on the market. You can get years of service on a dual-purpose, open-track, or club racer with this system. StopTech also makes a really good brake upgrade. It features 13-inch

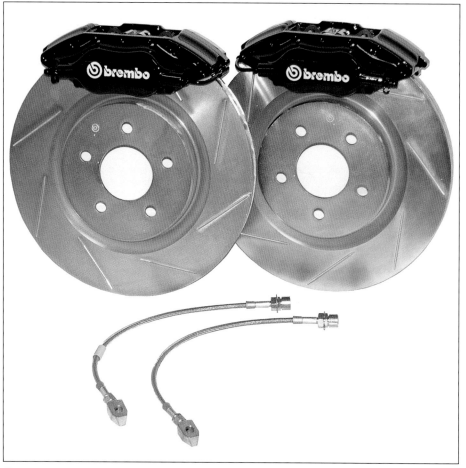

The 2000 Mustang Cobra R brake package (by Brembo) is available through Ford Racing. It's a very good brake upgrade kit at a reasonable price.

rotors, all the goodies included, for a couple of grand. Brembo makes a 14-inch brake upgrade with two-piece rotors, four-piston calipers, priced in the mid $3,000 range.

A number of Grand Am Cup teams are using the Wilwood six-piston calipers, but Wilwood also has a less-expensive street performance system. The street 13-inch rotor systems come with staggered piston sizes to equalize pad wear, two-piece rotors, and pads. The competition system has titanium pistons for maximum protection against heat, and competition series rotors. All of these brake upgrades require 17-inch or larger wheels with clearance for the calipers. The Cobra R-style wheel, Steeda Ultralite, or equivalent is a good choice when installing these brakes. Wilwood also makes an upgraded rear brake system to complement their SL6 front system using the Dynalite calipers, a 12.19-inch rear rotor, and an integral parking brake assembly. Many times, simply upgrading the rear brakes with slotted rotors and pads will complement a front system upgrade.

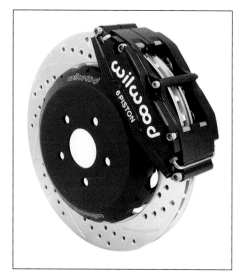

Wilwood 6-piston calipers and 13.5-inch vented rotors are a preferred brake package on Grand Am Cup Mustangs. A matching rear kit with integral parking brake is available. (Photo courtesy Wilwood)

Brake Cooling

Anytime a Mustang is running on a track for an extended period of time, getting cool air to the eye of the brake rotor is going to improve brake performance and longevity. The 2000 Cobra R came from the factory with carbon-fiber brake ducts in place of the standard backing plates. The front spoiler ducts channeled the air through tubes to the brakes.

This system, or similar systems available from the aftermarket, works wonders. The '03-'04 Cobra has an ideal location next to the fog lamp to duct cold air through, and the bumper cover can be retrofitted to older models too. Failing that, aftermarket ducts are available to pick up the air just below the bumper cover and direct it to the brake duct. Brake duct kits for the Mustang are available through Sean Hyland Motorsport and Kenny Brown. Any serious open-track car should incorporate some duct system to help keep the brakes working efficiently.

Brake duct hose must be wire or fabric reinforced and specifically designed to withstand temperatures up to 300 degrees F.

Drag Brakes

Drag racecars have their own unique requirements and challenges in the brake department. In addition to braking performance, weight is an issue – reducing front-end weight in particular. Another issue for drag racers is the front wheel size. Drag racers typically want to install a skinny 15 x 4-inch wheel on the front with a lightweight front-runner tire. These wheels do not fit an SN95 Mustang with Cobra-style brakes because the wheel interferes with the caliper. One inexpensive solution is to fit '94-'98 Mustang GT calipers and rotors, which clear 15-inch wheels.

A more elegant solution is to install an aftermarket drag brake system such as the Aerospace drag brake kit. These kits include billet aluminum lightweight four-piston front calipers, lightweight rotors, and aluminum rotor hats. A similar system is also available from Aerospace for the rear brakes as well. You can lose 20 lbs or more installing a system like this. Although they're adequate for drag racing, these lightweight systems do not have a big enough rotor to dissipate heat from successive stops, and should not be used on street-driven cars.

Another thing drag racers like to do is install a manual rack and pinion to eliminate the weight of a power steering system. On the '96-up Mustangs, which utilize the power steering pump to provide brake system assist, another master cylinder must be installed to eliminate the hydro boost. A manual master cylinder kit includes a master cylinder and a

Carbon fiber brake ducts were original equipment on 2000 Cobra R. Forcing cool air ducted from the front of the car, through the eye of the rotor, dramatically reduces brake rotor temperatures.

A manual master cylinder and adapter block are often used on Mustang drag cars with aftermarket brakes to eliminate the power brakes and reduce weight. This is also required when converting a '96-up Mustang to a manual steering rack, since the power steering pump also supplies the hydroboost brake assist with hydraulic pressure.

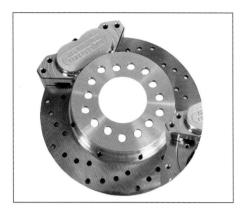

Left: Drag brake kits use very lightweight components, billet calipers, non-vented rotors, and aluminum rotor hats.

Brembo also offer their GT brake kit with two-piece floating 14-inch slotted and cross-drilled rotors for the Mustang. The larger 4-piston caliper requires 18-inch wheels for clearance.

Ducting air to cool the brakes can be done with a fabricated inlet riveted to the spoiler (above), or attached under the front valance. The 2003 Cobra front fascia (below) has a convenient unused air inlet that works fine for ducting air to the brakes. The Cobra fascia can be retrofitted on other models, as on this 2001 GT.

billet adapter to connect the master to the firewall. The master cylinder pushrod must be modified in most cases, and the pedal ratio may need to be increased in order to have sufficient line pressure to slow the car properly. This is a job best left to a professional shop.

When installing custom brake packages, particularly on drag race and road-race cars, we often eliminate the stock proportioning valve from the system, which limits the pressure applied to the rear brakes. As the weight transfers forward during braking, the load on the rear tires becomes less, and if the rear brake pressure is too high, the rear brakes lock up. This is not a good situation. An adjustable proportioning valve is used on custom brake installations to allow the driver to manually adjust the rear brake pressure to the desired level. On a drag car, this adjustment can usually be made and then left alone unless some change is made to the chassis or brake system. On a road-race car, the driver may adjust the proportioning valve during the race to compensate for fuel load, tire wear, or changing track conditions. A proportioning valve is only used on the rear brakes to limit the amount of brake force; it cannot increase the brake force above the output from the master cylinder, which is a function of the bore diameter of the master cylinder and the pedal ratio. We always want the front brakes on our Mustangs to lock up before the rears – always

A brake proportioning valve reduces the line pressure to the rear brakes, allowing the driver to adjust the brake balance front-to-rear to suit conditions.

When you're combining an aftermarket wheel with aftermarket brakes, fitment can be a leap of faith. Talk to some experienced installers to get some answers.

– no matter what we use the car for. Locking up the rear brakes first is a sure fire way to go off the track backwards, which is not usually the best plan.

Roll Control

Roll control is simply an electric solenoid placed in the front brake system, actuated by a button near the driver. When at the drag strip, the driver applies the brakes, activates the roll control with a momentary switch, and releases the brake pedal. The driver can spin the rear tires, heating the slicks or drag radials to optimum temperature, while the front brakes hold the car in place.

This method creates less wear and tear than holding the brakes on all four corners and overpowering the rear brakes. Installing a roll control on an ABS-equipped SN95 Mustang requires two roll controls, one for each front brake line. They must be installed after the line exits the ABS block in the right front of the engine compartment. As

The standard rear discs on the SN95s may not look like much, but remember, most earlier Mustangs came with rear drums.

The ultimate brakes. Parachutes are used to slow racecars to a speed where the hydraulic brake can take over.

with all serious brake work, this is a job best left to an experienced shop.

Parachutes

Well, parachutes are a supplemental brake system! Nothing says fast like a parachute hung on the back of your car. NHRA requires a parachute on any car capable of 150 mph in the quarter mile. They are also extensively used in speed trials at places like Bonneville. A parachute system is designed to work for a specific speed range and type of use. The main chute can be deployed by a spring system, or fired off with a CO_2 charge, and can be configured in many different ways. If a drag car or Bonneville car gets out of shape at speed, deploying the chute can be an effective method to get the car under control again, pulling back on the rear of the car and providing a stabilizing effect.

Once a racecar starts exceeding 200 mph on a regular basis, the parachute acts as a primary brake system, slowing the car to the point that the hydraulic brake system can operate. The lightweight brake systems used in drag cars are not going to work effectively at 200+ mph. If your project is fast enough to require a parachute, you need to contact the manufacturer for specific recommendations for your application.

Engines: 3.8L, 5.0L, & 5.8L

3.8L

More than 75 percent of all the SN95 Mustangs were equipped from the factory with the 3.8L V-6. Producing 145 hp in its 1994 form, this powerplant is usually overlooked by enthusiasts in favor of its larger and more-powerful siblings – the pushrod and overhead cam V-8s. And yet, there are some hardcore enthusiasts who've pushed development on the V-6 and offer some guidance for those who might follow in their steps. Tom Morana of Morana Racing Engines in Toronto is a leading proponent of the 3.8L V-6. His credentials include building a 12-second V-6 '84 Mustang all the way back in 1990 at a time when a V-8 was the only fashionable way to go fast. Morana has devoted his time for the past 20 years to squeezing big horsepower out of a small package.

The early 3.8L blocks used in the '94-'95 Mustang are adequate for moderate performance, but if you are after more than 300 hp or are using a supercharger, turbo, or nitrous oxide, the '96-up V-6 block offers some improvements. Chief among these are deeper holes for the head bolts on the intake side of the deck. The early blocks used holes that weren't as deep as the exhaust-side head-bolt holes, and the threads start at the deck surface instead of deep within the block. When the head bolts are torqued, the deck surface pulls up a slight amount, unloading the head gasket on the intake side of the deck. This feature, and poor-quality head gaskets, are contributing reasons for head-gasket failures on the early 3.8Ls, which they acquired a reputation for. The block was reconfigured in 1996, allowing deep threaded holes to anchor the inner head bolts in the same way that the outer ones had been anchored all along. The later block also has more support around the bottom of the cylinder bore, and the main caps are beefier as well.

Speaking of main caps, one of the weak points on the 3.8L is the 2-bolt main cap. Once you exceed 300 hp, the caps tend to move around, causing reliability issues. The solution is to use ARP main bolts and one of Tom Morana's stud girdles. The steel stud girdle ties all the main caps together, preventing flex.

Tom Morana – the V-6 engine master. Tom has nearly 40 years of engine building experience, and his shop, Morona Racing, specializes in the 3.8L.

The 3.8L V-6 bottom end needs help over 300 hp. The steel stud girdle and ARP studs add strength to main caps.

This simple fix ensures reliability at over 400 hp and 7,000 rpm.

All the 3.8L V-6 engines used in the Mustang come with a cast crankshaft. Power junkies who want to make more than 350 hp should consider using the crankshaft used in the Super Coupe T-Bird. The steel crankshaft used in the Super Coupe is much stronger, but there is a catch. The rear main journal is .010 inch smaller than the other mains. The easy solution is to grind the other journals down to the same size, allowing you to use a set of off-the-shelf .010-inch undersize main bearings. Federal Mogul or Clevite premium quality bearings should be used in all performance-oriented 3.8L engine buildups.

The standard 3.8L cast connecting rods are useable for moderate perform-ance applications, but they aren't con-sidered reliable past 5,500 rpm and 300 hp. The '94-'95 engines use a shorter connecting rod than the '96-up engines, the longer rod allowing a raised pin in the pistons, and a lighter assembly. After-market rods are available for the 3.8L from Scat and others. These need to be matched with the correct compression distance on the piston (the distance between the centerline of the piston pin and the top of the piston) and dish vol-ume in order to achieve the desired compression ratio. Forged pistons are available from JE and others to suit a variety of applications.

Increasing the displacement of the 3.8L is as easy as dropping in the longer stroke crankshaft from the larger 4.2L V-6. This cast crank increases stroke from the stock 3.39 inches to 3.74 inch-es. Of course, the rod length and piston compression distance must be matched to the increased stroke. Morana has forged rods and pistons that work well. For those who require even more, Tom has experimented with 4.4L and even 4.6L derivatives by offset grinding the crankshaft. However, reducing the diam-eter of the rod journals makes the crank more flexible and ultimately less robust, so it's best to stick with the 4.2L and to limit the RPM, respecting the cast-iron material it is constructed with.

When boring the block oversize to fit larger pistons, the bore can be increased from the stock 3.810 inches to a maximum of 3.875 inches. Larger bore sizes than this weaken the block and cause reliability issues. The oiling

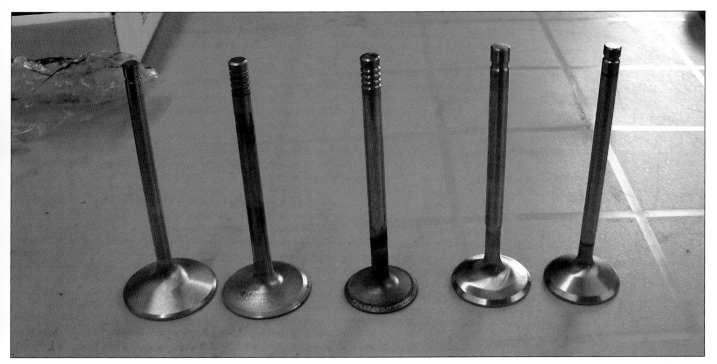

Compare these race valves on left – 2.02-inch intake, 1.60-inch exhaust – with the street performance valves on the right – 1.89-inch intake, 1.55-inch exhaust. That's a production exhaust valve in center.

system on the 3.8L has no inherent problems, and the standard pump, pick-up tube, and pan suffice for most performance applications. A high-volume pump is available from Speed Pro to increase oil supply.

Moving upstairs, two cylinder-head variations for the 3.8L V-6 are available. The early '94-'95 engines had a single intake port, while the later '96-2004 engines had a Siamese intake port with two runners feeding one intake valve. One runner supplies the cylinder with air at low RPM, and then the secondary port kicks in extra air at higher RPM. The timing of this addition is managed by the EEC-IV engine management system.

In 1996, the deck surface of the cylinder head was changed, providing more material around the bore, improving head gasket sealing. For performance use, the best head gasket to use is the Corteco gasket. It's an MLS design, incorporating an outer layer of steel, with an inner core of copper. The flexibility built into the head gasket means no more reliability problems from shift-

ing head gaskets. The stock head bolts are torqued-to-yield, one-time-use bolts and should be replaced with ARP bolts which increase clamp load on the gasket, enhancing the sealing qualities. Using all these techniques eliminates head gasket problems associated with the 3.8L V-6 for once and for all.

Increasing airflow in the cylinder heads via porting and larger diameter valves readily increases the power output of the 3.8L. The stock single-port '94-'95 cylinder heads flow 175 cfm on the intake port and 135 cfm on the exhaust port. These flow figures can be improved to 240 cfm on the intake and 180 cfm on the exhaust with porting. The stock '94-'98 valve sizes are 1.782 inches for the intake valve, and 1.4 inches on the exhaust side. '99-2004 engines come with 1.861-inch intake valves and 1.461 inches on the exhaust side. The best choice for a street engine is to upgrade to larger stainless-steel performance valves, 1.84 inches on the intake side, and 1.55 inches for the exhaust. These can be installed using the stock valve seat. All-out race engines can go as large as 2.02-inch intake and 1.60-

inch exhaust valves with larger diameter seats. The production valves have a stem diameter of .341 inch, and replacement stainless valves with smaller .312- or .275-inch stems help produce higher airflow in the ports. The later '96-up twin port heads can be ported to provide up to 270 cfm on the intake side.

The stock intake manifold and throttle body inhibit the flow into the intake ports, as the runners are too small to support the airflow potential of a modified cylinder head. Street engines can benefit from porting the stock upper and lower intake manifold, either by hand or using the Extrude Hone process, where an abrasive putty is forced under pressure through the ports. Extrude Honing increases the cross section of the runners and contours the curve of the runner at the same time. Another method for the upper intake is to cut open the intake through the plenum portion, port the runners from both sides, and then tig weld the intake back together. Radically reworked intake manifolds or custom sheet metal intake manifolds are required by the most extreme engines, to provide

Check out the racing double valvespring on left, the late production beehive spring in middle, and the single performance spring with titanium retainer on right.

This double roller timing chain kit has a 9-position crank gear to dial in camshaft advance and retard.

adequate airflow to support reworked cylinder heads. The stock throttle body, which has a 46-mm throttle-blade diameter, can be bored oversize and fitted with a 53-mm throttle blade. or a new 70 mm throttle body, available from BBK for the '01-'04 cars, can be fitted.

The 3.8L comes with a hydraulic-roller camshaft from the factory. Very few camshaft companies produce aftermarket grinds for the V-6, and COMP Cams recently joined the list. But worry not. Tom Morana has several profiles available that he regrinds on stock cores. His mild A38 camshaft has .480 inch of lift with the stock 1.73:1-ratio rocker arms. A larger B38 camshaft lifts the valves .519 inch with the 1.73:1 ratio rockers, or you can substitute 1.80:1 rocker arms, which boosts valve lift up to .540 inch. In fact, replacing the stock rocker arms with the 1.80:1 rockers is a good bolt-on performance increase for mildly tuned engines. The reground camshafts come with new pushrods to correct the valvetrain geometry for their reduced base-circle diameter. Tom has successfully used cams with up to .700 inch of valve lift in competition 3.8L engines.

The stock '94-'95 cylinder heads come with a single valve spring with an inner damper, while '96-up engines come with a conical spring. The stock seat pressure is 65 lbs. Performance camshaft profiles require increased rate valvesprings, and both heavy-duty single and double springs are available. A double spring combination, complete with aluminum retainer, typically gives 100 to 125 lbs of seat pressure, depending on installed height, and 350 lbs open pressure at .540 inch of valve lift. Engines with proper valvesprings and forged connecting rods can safely produce power over 7,000 rpm all day long.

Morana Racing Engines has produced its own double-roller timing chain kit to enhance high-RPM performance. The crank gear has a nine-position indexing feature, allowing the engine builder to dial in the camshaft

This 3.8L V-6 gets a little help from a ProCharger centrifugal supercharger.

timing to suit his/her requirements. There's a balance shaft located directly above the camshaft in the block. It is driven off the camshaft. This reduces vibration, particularly below 4,000 rpm. There is no performance benefit to removing the balance shaft, and it causes no grief at higher RPM, so it's best just to leave it alone and let it do its job.

In addition to the 3.8L V-6 internals, some bolt-on parts are available. The stock tubular exhaust headers are adequate for most street performance cars, but need to be augmented with a free-flowing exhaust system. Some manufacturers offer V-6 systems, or you can install a dual exhaust system designed for a V-8 powered Mustang and have your local muffler shop fabricate pipping between the headers and the cat-back

system. Larger capacity mass-air meters from the V-8 Mustangs, larger fuel injectors, and 255-lph fuel pumps should be added as the power output increases. The same fuel pumps and air meters that fit V-8 cars for a given year also fit the V-6 cars. Tuning software is available from both Superchips Custom Tuning and DiabloSport. With it, dyno shops across the country can tune your combination for best power and reliability. Search your local area, relying on customer referrals, for a competent tuner to dial in your package. It will be the best money you spend on the car, the finishing touch to a lot of time and effort, so don't scrimp in this department.

Some power adders are also available for the V-6. ATI Procharger and Vortech both offer supercharger kits with

up to 11 psi of boost. The Procharger kits include either a two- or three-core air-to-air intercooler, which is essential for producing reliable, consistent power with a blower. Simply bolting a basic seven-psi system on the V-6 yields up to 350 hp, and adding more boost on a built engine is the quickest way to build more power. Successful blown V-6 engines have produced in excess of 600 hp with the right components. The 3.8L can also benefit from a nitrous oxide system. However, since no 3.8L-specific kits are available, a universal system is required. NOS has universal EFI systems that are adaptable to the V-6 engine.

In the past, it was unusual to see a V-6 Mustang built to go fast. Thanks to people like Tom Morana, it's no longer

Kenny Brown used a 4.2L V-6 to make a very successful track car. The lighter weight of the V-6 engine produced a better-balanced package.

uncommon to see 11-second V-6 Mustangs prowling the streets. The only thing cooler than the smile on the owner's face is the disbelieving look of the V-8 Camaro driver after being spanked by a six-holer.

5.0L

The ubiquitous 302 engine, renamed the 5.0L in the Fox-body days, was in its most highly developed form in the '94-'95 Mustang. The small-block Ford pushrod engine, in production since 1963, was produced 240 hp in the '94-'95 Mustang Cobra. With thirty years of development by both Ford and the aftermarket, the array of performance parts available for this engine is mind-boggling. The production 5.0L engine as delivered in the '94-'95 Mustang GT produced 215 hp and 285-ft-lbs of torque with sequential fuel injection.

Increasing the power output of the 5.0L is a straight forward process. Since the 5.0L is already endowed with prodigious amounts of low-RPM torque, improving its ability to breathe at higher RPM pays dividends in the horsepower department. Long-tube headers add considerable power, especially if combined

with additional modifications to improve induction efficiency. Any header upgrade needs to be combined with an efficient mid-pipe and cat-back system. Depending on taste, a variety of aftermarket exhaust systems exist, each with their own sound, from the throaty hollow Trans Am sound of the Flowmaster mufflers to the almost European sound of the Magnaflow systems.

Headers with 1-5/8-inch primary tubes provide adequate flow for most street cars, while street/strip and competition cars can benefit from 1-3/4-inch primary tubes. The cat-back system is 2-1/2 inches in most cases, and matching diameter X or H pipes should be used in between. High-performance catalytic converters cost virtually no power, and should be used on all street-driven cars. Some owners prefer shorty headers, which retain more ground clearance and are easier to install. The break point as to which style of header you choose should be the total desired power output. A naturally aspirated engine utilizes the exhaust pulses to draw in additional air during the camshaft overlap period. Equal-length, long-tube headers produce the most effective exhaust

scavenging and hence the strongest pull through to the intake side, making more power. A supercharged engine is less sensitive in this respect, having the intake charge forced in, rather than relying on the exhaust pulse during camshaft overlap to help draw in the intake charge. Any 5.0L expected to produce in excess of 325 flywheel hp should have good quality long-tube headers. Hooker, Edelbrock, and Kooks all manufacture quality long-tube headers for the 5.0L.

Once we have the exhaust flowing efficiently, we can look upstream to increase intake efficiency. The stock airbox can be replaced with a more efficient design with a low-restriction air filter and a larger diameter air tube. C&L, Steeda, and MAC are just a few manufacturers that make cold-air kits for the '94-'95 Mustang 5.0L. Once the air inlet duct and filter are upgraded, the next restriction in the inlet system is the mass-airflow (MAF) meter. The '94-'95 Cobra already comes equipped with a larger 70-mm mass air meter. The '94-'95 Mustang GT comes with a 55-mm MAF, which must be replaced if the desired power output is more than 300 hp. The larger Cobra MAF is designed for 24-lb/hr injectors, so you need to add a set if you step up to the Cobra meter.

The '94-'95 Cobra engine also has a different intake manifold and cylinder heads than the GT engine. The breathing ability of the GT-40 cylinder heads, equipped with 1.84-inch intake and 1.54-inch exhaust valves, combined with the cast aluminum version of the GT-40 intake, provided additional airflow for increased power output. This is the point where GT and Cobra owners have different needs. GT owners want to replace the cylinder heads with higher-flowing ones. Ford Racing offers the aluminum GT-40 cylinder heads, upper and lower GT-40 EFI intake, inlet adapter, matching 65-mm throttle body, and 1.7 ratio rockers. This is a pretty good package for many street cars. Since these are production-based parts, you know they fit properly, and with some decent headers and exhaust, you're going to see 300 hp at the flywheel.

GT owners with upgraded heads and '94-'95 Cobra owners can bump the power level some more simply by adding a more aggressive aftermarket camshaft. Adding the 50-state-legal Ford Racing M-6250-E303 camshaft bumps the power output to 340 hp and still offers good street manners for an everyday car. At this point, we're getting pretty close to the end of the road as far as the airflow potential of the stock Cobra intake, so higher power output requires an intake and cylinder-head combo with more power potential. Achieving 400 to 500 hp with a naturally aspirated 5.0L requires a cylinder head/intake/camshaft combination that breathes efficiently to 6,500 rpm. Ford Racing offers their "Z" heads, which use 2.02-inch intake and 1.60-inch exhaust valves to flow 277 cfm through the intake port and 218 cfm through the exhaust at .550 inch of valve lift. These heads have a raised exhaust port and therefore require custom headers from someone like Kooks. Combined with an Edelbrock RPMII or Trick Flow Track Heat intake

Rebuilding your engine is an expensive and time-consuming project. Sometimes it's more cost effective to just install a new long block, like this Ford Racing 345-hp 5.0L with aluminum GT40 heads. (Photo courtesy Ford Racing)

The 347-ci stroker kit is a very popular option for increasing the displacement on the 5.0L engine. You can add cubic inches and stronger parts at the same time. (Photo courtesy Ford Racing)

manifold and an Accufab 75-mm throttle body, the Z heads can flow enough to achieve 400+ hp. Radical street engines, or street/strip/open-track cars could use a Ford Racing Z303 camshaft with .552 inch of valve lift and 228 degrees duration at .050. This camshaft has a rough idle and is marginal for a daily driver.

So far we have only discussed the top half of the engine, but now it's time to look at the bottom. The production short block is adequate to close to 400 hp and 6,000 rpm. Above there, the rods and pistons need to be replaced with forged components for durability. The production rod bolt is the weak link in the stock bottom end for high RPM, but Manley, Ford Racing, and others offer forged rods with ARP rod bolts that provide a trouble-free service life. Forged pistons of every conceivable type are readily available from JE, Manley, and others. The production nodular cast-iron crankshaft is quite adequate to well beyond 500 hp.

Whether you assemble your own engines or are depending on a professional to do it for you, quality machine work is required when fitting new components. Ask around your area and find the people with experience and knowledge on your specific application. Some shops specialize in drag race engines, others in road race work, and others in mainly stock rebuilds. Other Mustang enthusiasts can be a source of information, directing you to shops in your area. Ask the shop for the names of customers who have used their services, and check out the shop with the customers. It's easier to find a shop with experience in your particular area of interest than to have your engine become an R&D project.

If you're going to rebuild your 5.0L, it makes sense to increase the displacement with a stroker kit. Boring the block .030-inch oversize and increasing the stroke with an aftermarket 3.40-inch crankshaft turns your 302 into a 347. With the cost of parts coming down all the time, it's hardly more expensive than

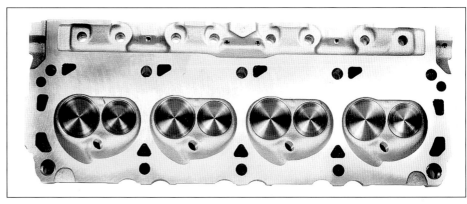

Bolt-on integrated packages, such as the Ford Racing GT-40 package, offer an easy solution to upgrading the engine in a street driven '94-'95 Mustang. These high-flowing GT-40 aluminum heads are the cornerstone of the package. (Photo courtesy Ford Racing)

The Ford Racing GT-40 EFI intake manifold has tubular runners for extra flow over the cast piece, plus it looks great. (Photo courtesy Travis Thompson)

upgrading your 302 components. Many 347 strokers have been built, and they seem to work well for street, drag, or track use.

There are a few other details that you'll want to attend to when building your engine. Although the 5.0L isn't especially noted for oiling troubles, a high-volume oil pump and a hardened oil pump driveshaft should be used for drag and open-track engines. A Moroso or Canton high-capacity oil pan, baffled for oil control, should be used on any serious open-track/road-racecar. An underdrive front pulley kit, always a popular bolt-on addition, slows the water

Many 5.0L intake manifolds were designed primarily for the '86-'93 5.0L (Fox-body), not the '94-'95. You can either find a manifold meant for the '94-'95 (left) or with a dog-leg adaptor (right) to put the throttle body in the right spot. (Photos courtesy Travis Thompson)

This 5.0L 65-mm throttle body lets more air into your intake manifold. Whether or not you need that extra air depends on the rest of your combination. (Photo courtesy Travis Thompson)

Large-diameter shorty headers are alright for street cars, but where maximum power is required, long-tube headers perform best. (Photo courtesy Ford Racing)

pump, preventing high-RPM cavitation on the road course. Cavitation means the water pump is turning so fast that the impeller can no longer grab water as it rotates, so the coolant flow inside the engine stops. Additionally, support systems like fuel pumps, injectors, lines, rails, and ignition systems need to be upgraded to keep pace with increased power output. Generally, 24-lb/hr injectors and an aftermarket 255-liter per hour replacement fuel pump will suffice to just under 400 hp. Above that, an aftermarket external fuel pump, regulator, billet fuel rails, and larger injectors (with a corresponding mass air meter and custom computer tune) are required. It's always good to plan where you ultimately want to end up with your project so you don't end up spending money twice, upgrading systems to one level, and then again to another level later on.

Supercharging is another way to increase the power output of your '94-'95 5.0L Mustang without necessarily tearing into the engine. Kits are available from ATI, Vortech, and Kenne Bell, just to name a few. For less than $3,000, you can get a basic street kit with 6-psi output, which can increase the power output up to 100 hp. An optional intercooled kit reduces the incoming air charge temperature by over 100 degrees, allowing you to make more power, create less wear and tear on the engine components, and allow you to safely run more boost. For these reasons, I really recommend spending a bit more to get an intercooled kit.

NOS wet plate nitrous oxide systems for 5.0L engines can be jetted for a power increase of 150 to 300 hp. Injection plates are available to fit in between the upper and lower stock, GT40, Holley, and Edelbrock intakes. (Photo courtesy NOS)

More horsepower often requires increasing the capacity of the cooling system. This three-core aluminum radiator is an excellent upgrade over the factory unit. (Photo courtesy Fluidyne)

Centrifugal superchargers like this ProCharger are common for 5.0L Mustangs. They have gained popularity because they're relatively easy to install and afford. (Photo courtesy Travis Thompson)

ATI produces an intercooled D1SC kit for the '94–'95 5.0L that easily supports 500–600 hp for drag racing. While superchargers make excellent power adders for the street and drag racing, road racing tends to favor naturally aspirated engine combinations for durability reasons.

The least expensive way to go faster is to add nitrous injection. NOS has several systems specifically for the 5.0L engine. For about $600, you can bolt on up to 100 hp with an NOS dry nitrous system in a couple of hours. The system comes complete with everything required for installation, and with the basic 10-lb nitrous bottle, you can get five or six quarter-mile passes before it needs to be refilled. Larger bottles are available for more fun before having to top up. Beyond the entry-level dry system, a 150-hp dry system includes a fuel pump upgrade, and a 150- to 300-hp wet plate system that fits between the upper and lower portions of most popular 5.0L intake manifolds. Any nitrous kit that adds over 140 hp should only be used with upgraded forged pistons and rods. Aftermarket racing blocks are required once engine output exceeds 500 to 600 hp, so once again, it's good to plan the ultimate destination of your buildup in advance.

Increasing the cylinder pressure by supercharging or injecting nitrous oxide taxes the ignition system. Although the Ford TFI ignition does a great job, plug

One nice thing about the 5.0L cars is that you can install a set of headers rather easily. The job is quite a bit harder on later 4.6L cars. If you want your headers to last, choose a set that either ceramic coated, stainless steel, or both. (Photo courtesy Travis Thompson)

Increased cylinder pressure from supercharging and nitrous can tax the standard ignition system. Billet distributors and high-output coils upgrade the ignition system to keep pace with the higher voltage requirements and increased rpm. (Photo courtesy MSD and Travis Thompson)

The SN-95 Mustang has even been used as a pro rally car. Here is a '95 Cobra R running a rally stage.

Many teams raced the '95 Cobra R successfully, including the #20 Steeda car, which won several races.

wires, coils, cap, and rotor should be upgraded with performance items, ensuring that an adequate amount of current is delivered to the spark plug. In general, you should go with spark plugs that are one or two heat ranges colder with power adders, and the plug gap should be reduced to .035 inch to ensure a consistent spark. We've had good success using NGK copper plugs in most of our power-adder projects.

5.8L

When Ford decided to build a homologation run of 250 1995 Cobra Rs, they decided that using the 5.0L engine would be like bringing a knife to a gun-fight. Ford needed the Cobra R to be powerful enough to have success against the hordes of 1LE Camaros and Porsche 968s that were running rampant at the time. And so, they dug through the parts bin and came up with a 5.8L marine short block, fitted it with GT-40 heads, and topped it with a cast Cobra intake manifold. Power output was 300 hp and 365 ft-lbs of torque. By the time the race teams were done massaging the engines to the letter of the rulebook, they were making more like 375 hp on 100-octane race fuel. Only 250 1995 Cobra Rs were built, and at the time, you could only purchase one if you held a competition license, the intent being to make sure the

cars got into the hands of racers and not collectors. The '95 Cobra R became quite successful in the hands of private race teams, winning many races until development of the 4.6L Cobra engine exceeded the 5.8's capability.

The '95 Cobra R came powered by this 5.8L pushrod engine. Its taller deck height required a cowl hood and a unique intake to fit. The owner of this Cobra R runs it in American Iron and AV8SS races. (Photo courtesy Travis Thompson)

The Modular Years

In 1996, Ford's venerable 5.0L pushrod engine became a victim of tightening emission requirements. The 4.6L modular V-8, first used in 1992 in the Crown Victoria sedan, became the base engine in the Mustang GT. At 215 hp and 285 ft-lbs of torque, the base V-8 engine was initially a disappointment to the Mustang enthusiasts weaned on the 5.0L and its prodigious low-RPM torque. The Cobra engine arrived with 305 hp

and 320 ft-lbs of torque, but again, the power was much higher in the RPM band than the Mustang drivers were accustomed to. It took just a little while (about a day for some) for the aficionados to realize that the modular engine was okay; it just needed a higher axle ratio to best utilize the available power. A set of 4.10:1 gears absolutely transforms a stock Cobra, and the lower-revving 2-valve GT worked well with 3.73:1. Once everyone

caught on that the 4.6L had to be wound out to near redline to really go, and a few of us showed its potential, the naysayers were quiet.

4.6L development escalated quickly after it became apparent that the 4-valve Cobra heads flowed as much air in stock form as a really good set of aftermarket 5.0L heads. Bolting on a centrifugal supercharger could boost the output of a stock Cobra engine from 305 to over 450 hp. Unfortunately, we discovered early on that some of the components, specifically the rods and pistons, weren't up to the task of taking on more horsepower.

At the same time, we were developing better components, creating air-to-air intercoolers for the supercharger kits, and gaining experience with improving the naturally aspirated 4.6 engines, first for SCCA showroom stock racing, and then developing a 5.0L big bore version of the Cobra engine beginning in 1997 for Motorola Cup endurance racing. In just over 2-1/2 years, from the time the 1996 Cobra came out, we were able to extract over 800 hp from the 4.6L 4-valve engine for drag racing and 380 hp from the 5.0L road-race engine – using stock heads and intake! With the potential of the 4.6L engines now clear for everyone to see, it wasn't long before others joined the fray. Although they were initially more expensive to work on, 4.6L engines established themselves as being more

This is the complete 320-hp 4.6L DOHC engine as it came in 1999 and 2001 Cobras. It features more traditional single intake ports, unlike the 305-hp DOHC that came in 1996-1998 Cobras, which has two intake ports per cylinder.

cost effective in some respects. Where the stock 5.0L block was prone to failure at over 600 hp, the production 4.6L iron block has been reliable at 900 hp, and the 4.6L aluminum block is capable of 1,600 hp! No production North American V-8 block I am aware of is in this league. Ford certainly over-engineered many aspects of the modular V-8 design. The overhead cam valvetrain is capable of 9,600 rpm with very limited modifications. So, let's see what we can do with this package, shall we?

2-Valve 4.6L

The 2-valve 4.6L base engine for the Mustang GT arrived with 215 hp at 4,400 rpm, but its restrictive cylinder heads ran out of breath at 5,000 rpm. This resulted in a narrow powerband between 3,200 and 5,200 rpm where the engine really sang. Supercharging was the easiest way of overcoming this deficiency for the first three years until better cylinder heads became economically

available. In 1998, Ford Racing released a high-performance 2-valve cylinder head, along with a matching high-flow intake manifold (sometimes referred to as the SVO heads and intake). This cylinder-head and intake-manifold combo is the best out-of-the-box package available today. With an appropriate camshaft upgrade, this package provides an effective powerband from 3,500 to 6,500 rpm. The M-6049-D46 heads flow 203 cfm at .550 valve lift through the intake port and 141 cfm at .550 on the exhaust side. The intake valves are 46.83 mm, while the exhaust valves are 35.88 mm. To improve flow, the valve centerlines were moved 2 mm to unshroud the intake valve. Combined with long-tube headers, underdrive pulleys, a cold-air inlet, and computer tuning, this cylinder head/intake combo on a stock '96-'98 short-block has produced over 350 hp on 91 octane pump fuel – not too shabby for 281 cubic inches.

In 1999, the Mustang GT was upgraded to 260 hp and 300 ft-lbs torque

Replacing the stock one-time-use head bolts and main bolts on the 4.6 with aftermarket studs is a good choice when rebuilding the engine.

via Power Improved (PI) cylinder heads, higher-lift cams, and a higher-flowing intake manifold. This upgrade substantially improved the GT's performance, and with the stock axle ratio upgraded to 3.27:1, the engine was operating in its powerband more of the time. Immediately, the affordable price of the production PI heads and intake allowed '96-'98 GT owners to upgrade their cars to 1999 power levels. This is still a very cost-effective ($1,500) upgrade, and also allows the owner a wider range of camshaft choices, as many of the aftermarket designs are only available for the higher-lift PI heads. The PI heads were redesigned to provide increased retainer-to-seal clearance, permitting higher camshaft lift.

Going downstairs for a moment, two versions of the 4.6L iron block are available. The Romeo block was used from 1996-1999. In 2000, due to capacity issues at the Romeo plant, some Mustangs came with Windsor engines, including a different block, minor differences in the cylinder heads, unique valve covers, and an eight-bolt crankshaft flange instead of the regular six-bolt crank flange used on the Romeo engines. The Windsor plant normally produced the 4.6L and 5.4L engines slated for duty in the F-series trucks, but due to overwhelming demand, it was tapped for extra capacity. Functionally,

In 1999, the 4.6L 2-valve engine received the power improved (PI) cylinder heads and intake, plus hotter cams, resulting in a power jump to 260 hp.

the engines are interchangeable, as long as some of the unique exterior dress is used, and we have built successful race and street engines using both blocks. The main bearings are different between the two blocks, and this is probably the most significant thing to be aware of when rebuilding these engines. The Windsor block has a "W" cast in the valley and on the front of the block under the timing cover.

Centrifugal superchargers have been popular on the 4.6L engines since the beginning. Power increases of 40 to 60 percent are common on stock engines. Higher power outputs require improved rods and pistons.

The 2001 Bullitt Mustang, which was based on the GT, came with a unique high-flow intake manifold, similar in design to the Ford Racing performance intake, but manufactured to mate up with the PI cylinder head intake ports. The Bullitt intake manifold added 5 hp and 15 ft-lbs of torque, but it's not significantly better than the production intake with an aftermarket throttle body and plenum. One might be able to justify the cost on an all-out 2-valve engine.

Accufab's John Mehovitz is a 4.6L pioneer and owner of the fastest 4.6L-powered drag car, which runs the quarter-mile at 6.62 seconds at 210 mph. Mehovitz had produced a 75-mm throttle body upgrade for the 4.6L 2-valve engine, but wouldn't release it because it only produced a 2 hp gain on a '99 Mustang GT. After some investigation, he

Accufab 75-mm throttle body and intake elbow bolts on an instant 11 hp.

Handheld programmers like this Diablo Predator allow the owner to adjust spark, fuel, and many other parameters in the engine-management computer. This tool allows the owner to optimize the calibration for all the modifications that have been made to the car.

determined that the throttle body elbow was the restriction in the inlet system, and with a new casting, gained a total of 11 hp on a stock PI engine with the throttle body/elbow combo. The stock PI intake with an Accufab throttle body/elbow is quite capable of producing 400 naturally aspirated horsepower – with ported cylinder heads, large valves, camshafts, and long-tube headers.

The NOS NOSzle system produces up to 300-hp gains on a prepared 4.6L 2-valve engine. Of course, you can run a smaller shot on a stock engine.

Other bolt-on items that deserve mention include underdrive pulley kits, cold-air induction, and of course, exhaust upgrades. Changing the original cat-back exhaust system is usually one of the first modifications a Mustang owner makes, if not for the power increase, certainly to obtain a more noticeable exhaust sound. Many excellent cat-back systems are on the market from companies such as Magnaflow, JBA, and Borla.

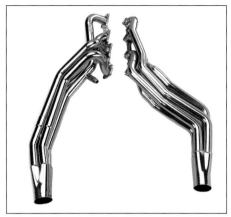

Hooker long-tube headers are popular performance modification for 2- and 4-valve Mustangs. Get them ceramic coated if you want them to survive the elements. (Photo courtesy Hooker)

Replacing the stock powdered-metal connecting rods with forged H-beam rods is among the first things we change in a high-output 4.6L. Ford included forged rods in the '03 and '04 supercharged Cobra engine.

A low-restriction cat-back system can be worth 5 hp or so on a GT. Substituting the original H-pipe for an aftermarket X- or H-pipe can pick up another 5 to 7 hp. Moving forward, replacing the stock exhaust manifolds with shorty headers from Ford Racing or JBA nets another 3 to 8 hp. A serious naturally aspirated engine package must use long-tube headers if the true power potential is to be exploited. A header with long primary tubes always produces more power than with a shorty header. A 1-5/8 primary tube diameter is okay up to about 340 hp, but a 1-3/4-inch primary out-performs the smaller tube diameter at higher power levels. A 2-1/2 diameter H- or X-pipe is sufficient up to 450 hp, at which point, a 3-inch diameter rear system provides gains. Hooker and JBA both produce some decent long-tube headers for the GT. Hardcore racers want

Adding nitrous on the '03-'04 Cobra's has become popular. NOS now offer a specific kit just for this application.

to get custom headers from Kooks to maximize their packages.

The production GT short block is capable of 400 to 450 hp with the stock components, so long as no detonation occurs. If you start rattling the engine with detonation, the stock hypereutectic pistons break first. The ring lands between the top and second rings crack from the sudden sharp pressure wave in the cylinder.

Forged pistons from Manley and JE are available in many different dish volumes, so you can tailor your compression ratio for your needs. Aftermarket pistons have the top ring land moved down to move the ring away from the extreme heat that can be generated with supercharger boost or nitrous use. The production powdered-metal rods have also proven fragile as power increases. Forged connecting rods are available from Manley and other manufacturers. H- and I-beam rods are available in configurations to handle up to 1,200 hp. Above that, we have our own custom 300M rods produced by Manley, which are durable at 1,600+ hp. The stock cast crankshaft handles 500 hp, but above that, we like to substitute the forged, fully counterweighted crankshaft used in the 4.6L Cobra engine. Race main and rod bearings from Federal-Mogul and main studs from ARP complete the short block upgrade.

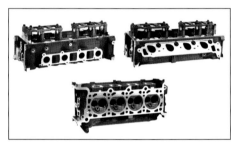

The Ford Motorsport M-6049-D46 cylinder head is the best flowing SOHC head available out of the box. (Photo courtesy Ford Racing)

The M-9424-E46 intake manifold is designed to work with the heads, which have a unique port shape, not compatible with the PI or Bullitt intake manifolds. (Photo courtesy Ford Racing)

In 2000, we pioneered the stroker kit for the 4.6L in a quest to make a 500-hp road-race engine with more midrange torque. Everyone has now seen the benefit of the stroker kit in the 4.6L, and the cost of substituting a stroker rotating assembly is so reasonable, more and more people are going with a stroker instead of a stock rebuild. With a 3.75-inch stroke, your 4.6L goes from 281 cubic inches to 302.

The oiling system can be readily upgraded with a high-volume oil pump and pickup tube from the Cobra, along with our billet oil-pump gears. The stock powdered-metal gears have been found to break under some types of vibration, causing immediate and catastrophic engine failure. The billet gears are just cheap insurance. The Cobra oil pan and windage tray are a good, inexpensive oil-pan upgrade, but aftermarket wet- and dry-sump pans are also available from Moroso and Canton.

The stock MLS head gaskets secured with ARP studs work fine for head-sealing up to over 800 hp. The Cobra timing chains can be used in the GT engine, and they are specially polished for higher-RPM duty. They are a worthwhile upgrade for a higher-rpm GT engine. The rest of the production 2-valve valve-train works dandy up to 6,500 rpm, above which, a spring upgrade from COMP Cams or Manley is recommended. The stock PI cams have .535 inches of lift, but only 192 degrees duration on the intake and 184 degrees on the exhaust side (both at 0.50 inch of lift). Aftermarket billet camshafts are available from COMP Cams, Crower, and Sean Hyland Motorsport. The stock PI head supports .550 inch of valve lift with no modifications. Mild street engines should look for cams with duration in the 210-220-degree range (at .050), while 230 to 245 degrees of duration is suitable for more radical cars. The choppy idle and poor low-RPM response typical with longer duration cams is amplified on the 4.6L because of its small displacement. If you're still working with original '96-'98 GT heads, the valve lift is limited to .500 inch due to the design. This isn't a problem because all

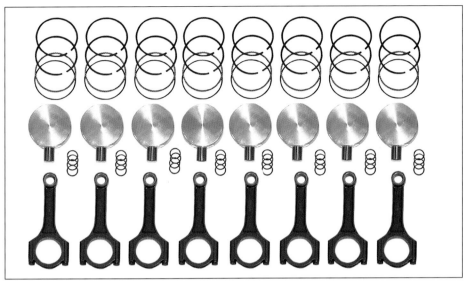

This stroker kit with 3.75-inch stroke is a popular upgrade when rebuilding the 4.6L. It bumps you up to 5.0L of displacement.

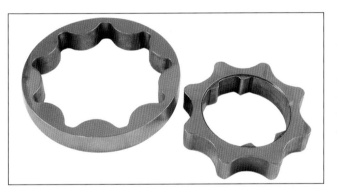

Billet oil pump gears are a must for reliability. The stock gears have been known to shatter, which will ruin your day.

This great illustration compares the valve-curtain area of the 2- and 4-valve cylinder heads. It explains why the 4-valve requires so much less lift.

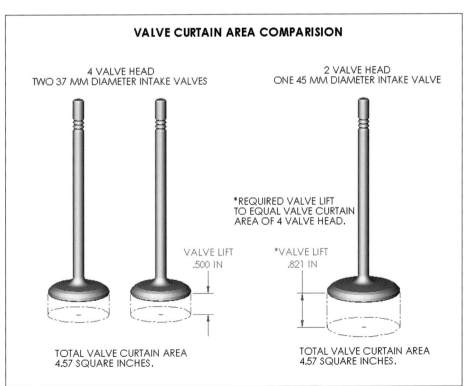

VALVE CURTAIN AREA COMPARISION

4 VALVE HEAD
TWO 37 MM DIAMETER INTAKE VALVES

2 VALVE HEAD
ONE 45 MM DIAMETER INTAKE VALVE

*REQUIRED VALVE LIFT TO EQUAL VALVE CURTAIN AREA OF 4 VALVE HEAD.

VALVE LIFT
.500 IN

*VALVE LIFT
.821 IN

TOTAL VALVE CURTAIN AREA
4.57 SQUARE INCHES.

TOTAL VALVE CURTAIN AREA
4.57 SQUARE INCHES.

the camshaft vendors offer specific cams with less lift just for the earlier heads.

The GT 2V engine can be readily upgraded to produce good streetable power, or twisted harder to make a decent race engine, but for big power, both naturally aspirated and with forced induction, you can't beat the 4-valve Cobra engine. The 4-valve's flow potential, because of its increased valve curtain area with two intake valves, makes it the hands-down winner.

4-Valve 4.6L

The '96-'98 Cobra heads have a twin-intake-port design, and are known as "B" heads. The intake ports are actually too big for the street, so one port was designated only for high-RPM use. This secondary intake port is used only above 3,000 rpm when the computer opens a set of throttle plates known as the intake manifold runner control (IMRC). Stock, these heads flow 231 cfm at .500 inch of valve lift on the intake and 145 cfm at .500 on the exhaust side. The stock intake manifold is tuned for best power at 6,000 rpm, so it runs out of steam above that, but if you add a supercharger, it keeps right on making power to redline. Bolt-ons for the '96-'98 Cobra include good long-tube headers from Hooker or Kooks, a cat-back exhaust, an X- or H-pipe, underdrive pulleys, and low-restriction cold-air inlets.

As with the GT engine, the basic 4-valve engine components are durable to 450 hp, above which, the rods and pistons need to be changed out. The Cobra engine already comes with a forged steel crankshaft, which we are still using even at 1,600 hp, albeit with some additional preparation. Unlike the iron GT blocks, which can only be bored .040-inch oversize maximum, the aluminum block is of Siamese bore construction. A Siamese block has material joining the adjacent bores, adding strength. In 1997, we pioneered sleeving the block oversize with thin-wall ductile iron sleeves to increase the bore diameter from 3.551 to 3.70 inches.

This gives us 5.0Ls of displacement, but besides the extra cubic inches, the larger bore diameter also unshrouds the intake valves, enhancing cylinder-head

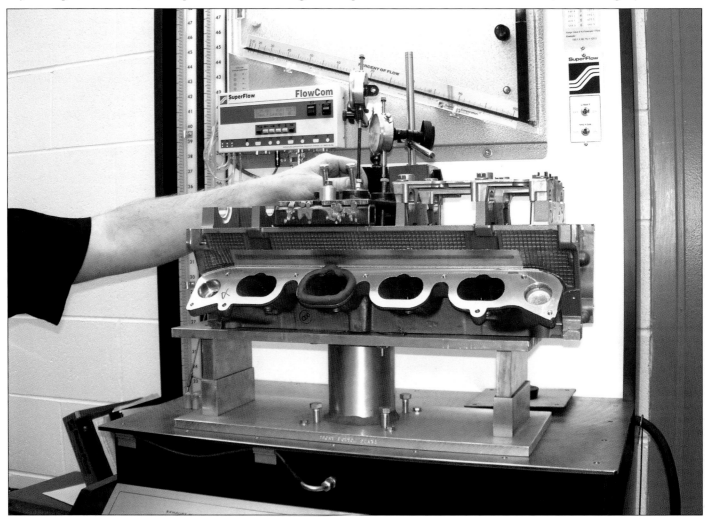

A 4-valve cylinder head is tested on a SuperFlow SF-600 flow bench following porting modifications. A good port job increases flow at all lift values.

flow. While this isn't the best route for a forced-induction setup, big-bore Cobra engines became extremely competitive against LS1 Camaros in professional road racing, winning numerous races in Grand Am Cup competition. The 5.0L big-bore package was also adopted for the Daytona Prototype class, and produces a reliable 500 hp with the Ford Racing FR500 cylinder heads and intake manifold.

This brings us back to cylinder heads again. In 1999, the Cobra came with a new head design, the tumble-port head, this time with a more conventional appearing intake port arrangement. The port was much smaller in size, but the low lift flow was improved over the B head, and it also made more low-end torque. Somewhere between engineering sign-off and production, the 1999 Cobra managed to lose some horsepower. The early production '99 Cobras were a little off of their 320-hp rating. A ported intake manifold and revised computer calibration brought the cars back to where they should have been. You can tell if your Cobra has the revised intake manifold by checking the inside of the lower intake. If it looks smooth, not rough as cast, then you have the upgraded intake. To fix the intakes, Ford used the Extrude Hone process, where an abrasive putty is forced through the intake under pressure, polishing the inside of the runners (where hands cannot readily get to). Later '99

Cobras and all '01 Cobras make good on their promise of 320 hp.

The '99-2001 tumble-port heads were an improvement, but it got better. In 2003, the Cobra and the Mach 1 received a new head design based on the tumble port, but with a revised short turn radius for improved flow. The intake port now flowed as much as the B series head at .500 inch of lift, and still matched the tumble port at low lift. More significantly, the exhaust port received a 15-percent flow increase. Early in the 2003 Cobra production run, engineers decided to upgrade the head in another fashion. Since the very beginning, the 4.6L heads had been cast as one single casting, and then machined for left and right banks. Because the water flows opposite directions through the casting on the left and right banks, the water flow is optimum in only one direction. With the supercharged engine in the '03 Cobra, the exhaust valves on the driver's side head were not being cooled as well as engineers would have liked. So, a dedicated left and right casting were produced, along with a revised head gasket. The Mach 1 received the same updated driver-side head in mid 2003.

The '03 and '04 4-valve Mach 1 is rated at 305 hp, and the cylinder heads work so well that just adding a set of long tube headers, cat back exhaust, and our mild Stage 1 camshafts are

enough to jump the power up to more than 390 hp! All this in a Mustang with a solid axle – what more could a guy ask for? The only aftermarket cylinder head for the 4-valve 4.6L engine is the Ford Racing FR500 cylinder head, and it's a good one. Out of the box, they outflow even the '03 Cobra head, and it's our first choice when we are building a high-horsepower naturally aspirated engine. The excellent Ford Racing FR500 intake manifold, which has both long and short runners, is the best manifold to use with these heads. The FR500's internal throttle plates are actuated by the computer to switch from one set of runners to the other, maximizing the power over a broad RPM range. While the heads and intake are not inexpensive, for open-track/road-race, they're the best way to make 500+ hp naturally aspirated.

As far as street cars go, all the 4-valve cylinder heads work pretty well, and adding some longer-duration camshafts and long tube headers really wakes these cars up. We have eight different camshaft profiles for the Cobra, from emission legal street cams to 1,600-hp turbo profiles. With Cobra cams, you can either put in new billet cams or exchange your set for reground camshafts, a less-expensive process that we have used for 10 years. The stock valvesprings are good for 7,200 rpm, but

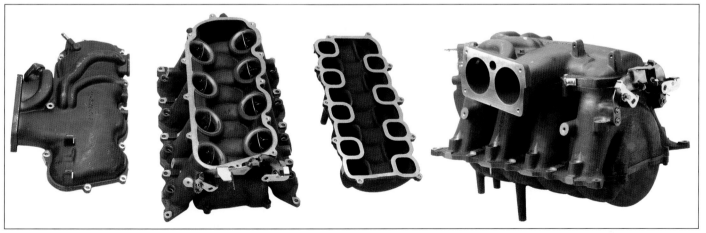

The Ford Racing FR500 intake manifold has a dual runner design – one set of long runners for low-RPM performance, and a second shorter set of runners for best power over 4,000 rpm.

Precision timing a set of race camshafts on a DOHC Cobra engine is a time-consuming but necessary process when building a performance 4-valve engine.

nally polish the entire crankshaft, and then shot peen and heat treat it for durability in road-race/open-track applications. The constant on-the-gas, off-the-gas nature of road racing is also hard on the oil pump gears, so I strongly recommend using billet oil-pump gears not only for road racing, but for any performance 4.6L buildup.

As with the GT, you can add a stroker crankshaft to your 4-valve 4.6L to make it a 5.0L. We originally developed a stroker crank in 2000 to compete with one of our customers in a higher road-racing class. Combined with a big-bore package, the displacement reached 5.2 liters, and we were able to achieve over 475 hp with production '99 tumble port heads and a radically reworked intake manifold. Today, the stroker crankshaft is a popular upgrade when rebuilding the Cobra or Mach 1 engines, especially if you're staying naturally aspirated. The main bearing clearances and alignment are especially critical in the aluminum block. The bearing clearances cold are just over .001 inch, so we find that every block needs to be align honed when rebuilt to achieve perfect results.

The OEM timing components on the Cobra/Mach 1 have proven to be quite robust, even at 9,000 rpm, but a couple of things need to be noted. The chain tensioners used from 1996 until 2001 had a ratchet mechanism built in to self-adjust the tensioner for wear. When drag raced on sticky tires, the tensioners would over ratchet, causing premature front cam-journal wear. We have modified the tensioners to eliminate the ratchet mechanism for drag racing, but kept it for street, open-track, or road racing. Since 2003, the factory has seen fit to update the tensioners and they have also eliminated the ratchet mechanism. They also changed the tensioner material from the original cast iron to a nylon-type material. We use the newer chain tensioner in street and drag cars, but we still use the old cast tensioners with the ratchet

we have a double-spring kit for racing engines, which has been used successfully to 9,600 rpm for drag racing and 8,000 rpm for endurance racing.

When preparing the Cobra aluminum block for output above 450 hp, the rods and pistons need to be changed

out for forged pieces. The factory forged crankshaft requires little more than balancing, unless the engine is to be road raced. We have experienced a couple of broken cranks in road-race engines over the years as a result of stress raisers left during the factory machining. We exter-

The forged steel 4.6L Cobra crankshaft (top) is manufactured with a center counterweight that provides improved performance at high RPM. The cast-iron 4.6L GT crankshaft (bottom) is suitable up to 500 hp and 6,500 rpm.

By swapping pulleys on an '03 or '04 Cobra, you can increases the output of the stock supercharger. Kits with interchangeable pulleys are available from the aftermarket.

mechanism for all road-race and open-track engines. The '96-'98 Cobra engines had a two-piece crankshaft gear which would occasionally fail on high-horsepower supercharged engines. This was updated to a single-piece gear in 1999, and we update every engine that comes apart to the newer specification. Another upgrade is the driver-side timing-chain guide, which was updated in 2001, following failures in the field. The newest design bolts through the oil pump with a longer bolt, supporting the lower two inches of the guide.

The factory crankshaft damper, water pump pulley, and alternator pulley can be exchanged for underdrive units that reduce parasitic losses and reduce the speed of the accessories. This is especially helpful for the water pump, which can cavitate at higher RPM, reducing cooling efficiency. Many of the aftermarket underdrive pulley kits on the market reduce the effectiveness of the damper, resulting in increased harmonics and contributing

to oil-pump-gear failures. Our newest design retains 92 percent of the original mass, reducing drag, but still providing adequate damping characteristics. The factory had a couple of different crankshaft bolts on the 4-valve over the years, and more than one torque specification. Since inadequate clamping load creates oil pump and crank gear problems, it's important to only use the black crank gear bolt (not the inferior silver one), replace the crank-gear-bolt every time it is removed, and torque it to 125 ft-lbs.

The 2003 Cobra was a landmark Mustang because it sold not only to the loyal Mustang enthusiasts, but it also crossed over, drawing in people who had previously never owned a Mustang. The car represented such a performance value that it appealed to everyone. The 390-hp iron-block 4-valve engine came from the factory with forged rods and pistons, and an intercooled Eaton supercharger. This engine can be easily make over 500 hp – with just bolt-on parts.

Owing to the conservative tuning of the OEM engine package, popular hot rodding techniques can provide impressive power increases. Changing the cat back system on a '03-'04 Cobra to a low restriction Magnaflow, Borla, or similar, adds 25 to 30 hp. A low-restriction cold-air inlet from Steeda or C&L picks it up another 20+ hp, and increasing the boost by 6 psi, to a total of 14 psi, with a pulley kit from Metco adds another 25+ hp. Combine some computer tuning with an SCT Excalibrator 2 or a Diablo Predator, and in no time you exceed 500 hp, without cracking the engine open. In fact, adding a Kenne Bell twin-screw supercharger upgrade with larger injectors, fuel rails, and an Accufab throttle body can boost the total output over 600 hp on pump fuel. The stock bottom end on the '03-'04 Cobra is so good, right from the factory, that the power can be increased to amazing levels for a stock engine.

Supercharging of the earlier-model Cobras remains one of the most popular ways to increase power. The stock cylin-

An air-to-air intercooler like this one from ProCharger is a great way to lower your intake charge temps with a centrifugal blower or turbocharger.

der-head flow potential is so good, yet held back somewhat with intake tuning designed to maximize midrange torque, that adding a supercharger results in impressive power output. The Vortech S-Trim was the first readily available centrifugal supercharger kit for the '96-'98 Cobra, and at only 8 psi, it would produce more than 450 hp.

Vortech's T-Trim became available in 1997, and we experimented with increasing the boost to over 15 lbs on engines with forged rods and pistons, ported heads, and camshafts. In no time, power output was in the mid-600-hp range, and every time we reached a new challenge to increase the power output, we just developed whatever was necessary. At first, we needed to cool the intake charge, as the discharge temperature of the T-Trim was over 300

This impressive-looking individual throttle body arrangement provides superior top-end power on this naturally aspirated drag car.

degrees F, which created tuning and durability problems. A prototype Vortech aftercooler did not have enough intercooler surface area to cool the intake charge, so we developed our own air-to-air intercooler. After four or five prototypes, we had one that would support 800+ hp, but the supercharger drive belt was slipping, so we had to develop an 8-rib supercharger drive system. Then we needed bigger fuel rails for more flow, larger injectors, etc., etc. – you get the idea.

Today, ATI, Kenne Bell, and Paxton all create intercooled street kits for the Cobra and Mach 1. They also have custom high-output race kits that can be assembled from various components.

You may also consider nitrous oxide for your Cobra. NOS has a couple of kits specifically engineered for the 4.6L. They offer a dry nitrous oxide system, adjustable from 75 to 150 hp, for both 2- and 4-valve engines.

NOS also has it's exclusive NOSzle system for the 4.6L 2-valve engine, which injects both nitrous and fuel in through a proprietary nozzle between the standard fuel injector and the intake manifold. This package comes complete with a plug-and-play wiring harness, control box, the works. It's a very nice package that can produce from 100 to 300 hp gains. There's also an NOS kit for '03-'04 Cobra with a wet plate system that fits between the throttle body and the intake manifold that can add up to 150 hp.

The ignition system is marginal on the 4.6L engines, particularly the '96-'98 cars, when adding nitrous and supercharging. The increased cylinder pressure can literally blow out the spark, causing loss of power. We have tried a number of solutions over the years, and the following recommendations are the result.

Change the OEM spark plugs for NGK TR6 copper core plugs, gapped to .030 inch, and add a set of MSD plug wires. On '96-'98 cars, upgrade ignition coils to ACCEL or MSD units, and use

an MSD DIS4 or Kenne Bell Boost a Spark to increase voltage. On the '99 and '01 Cobra, use the '03 Cobra coil-on-plug coils, because the early ones had issues. With these upgrades, the ignition systems can keep pace with the rest of the engine package. Likewise, with increased power comes the requirement for fuel pump upgrades, larger fuel injectors, larger capacity mass air units, and custom computer tuning. It's best to determine where you want to end up with your project first, and then upgrade to the required level in one step, so you don't have to replace components two or three times along the way.

5.4L Cobra R

The 2000 Cobra R, the second factory-built racecar in the SN95 lineage, came with a unique and very powerful engine package. The 5.4L Cobra R engine, rated at 385 hp, was all about racing. The short block contained forged Carillo rods, forged pistons, and a forged crankshaft. The cylinder heads were specific to the Cobra R,

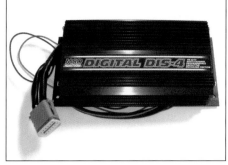

MSD DIS-4 ignition upgrade increases voltage at the spark plug and provides rev limit protection.

featuring a raised intake port, made possible by using a special short valve lash adjuster. The Cobra R heads are by far the best-flowing modular V-8 head ever built.

The intake port flows 268 cfm at .500 inch of valve lift, while the exhaust flows 206 cfm at .500 lift! The intake manifold is equally impressive, with long intake runners crossing over to the opposite side of the engine and a mammoth plenum chamber. Even the accessories were designed for racing, - the huge power steering and alternator pul-

Kenne Bell offers excellent supercharger kits for 2- and 4-valve engines. It's a great way to add over 100 hp – even with the base package.

The 2000 5.4L Cobra R engine is impressive looking – especially the large intake plenum. This engine came rated at 385 hp.

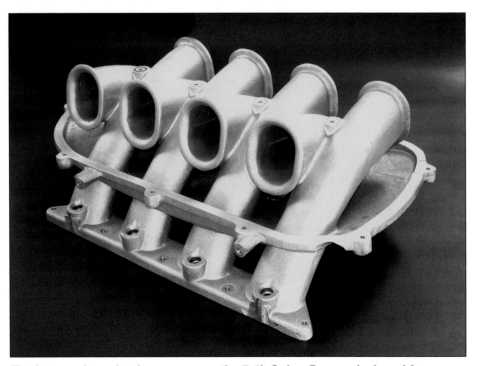

The large-volume intake runners on the 5.4L Cobra R were designed for maximum power and torque over a broad RPM band.

leys were designed to keep the accessory speeds within acceptable limits. The oil pan was fully baffled and had extra capacity for racing. Although the package was street legal, every advantage for racing was exploited within the allowable limits. The cars were sold directly from SVT dealers showrooms, and unlike the 1995 Cobra R, the purchaser was not required to have a competition license. Although the Cobra R and its unique engine package were designed to be raced, very few actually were.

The main issue for the Cobra R was and is lack of parts availability. The majority of special components used on the Cobra R, particularly the engine parts, i.e., heads, intakes, cams, etc., have never been available as spares, which makes it difficult to race one. A handful of Cobra Rs have been raced with some success, but the engine is certainly destined to be a rarity in the future.

Transmissions

The Mustang was available with four different manual transmissions between 1994 and 2004, depending on the engine and model year. Ford sourced these transmissions first through Borg Warner, which was purchased by the Mexico-based Tremec company in the mid 1990s. Initially, the 1994 and 1995 Mustangs were available with the T-5 5-speed transmission popularized in the Fox-body Mustang. The V-6 came with the T-5 through the '04 model year, but the 4.6L V-8 debuted in '96 with the T-45 5-speed transmission. The 4.6L Mustang received an upgraded 5-speed, the T-3650, beginning in mid-2000 model year. The 2000 Cobra R and the '03-'04 supercharged Cobra each used a different version of the T-56 6-speed transmission.

Automatic transmissions offered in the Mustang included the AODE on the '94-'95 Mustang, which evolved into the 4R70W electronic overdrive transmission used from '96 until '04 on the GT. The '03-'04 Mach 1 used an upgraded version of that transmission known as the 4R75W. So, now that you have the background, let's get inside them.

T-5 5-Speed

The T-5 5-speed manual overdrive transmission was used in '94-'95 5.0L V-8 cars and all V-6 cars from 1996 to 2004. The T5 has a separate bellhousing that can be removed from the main transmission case, unlike the T-45 where the bellhousing is an integral part of the transmission case. The input shaft has a 10-spline input, and the World Class V-8 transmission is rated at 335 ft-lbs torque capacity.

While reasonably robust, these transmissions can be prone to failure as power output is increased. In particular, third gear seems to fail when abused. The shift forks can get bent or broken from power shifts, and the synchronizer cones often get chipped or burred teeth from hard shifting. Some of these problems can be helped with a good aftermarket shifter, such as the ones manufactured by Steeda and Hurst. In addition to providing a shorter, more positive shift, adjustable shift stops allow the driver to bang home the gears without bending the shift forks. Serious drag race and open track types can now get dog-box conversions of the T-5. These upgraded transmissions have the stock synchronizers replaced with positive-engagement dog drives, just like custom race boxes have. Although impractical for the street, these do offer the ultimate in speed shifting potential, and are extremely durable in high-power situations. A number of transmission specialists are around now, such as G-Force and Liberty, who can handle T-5 rebuilds and upgrades.

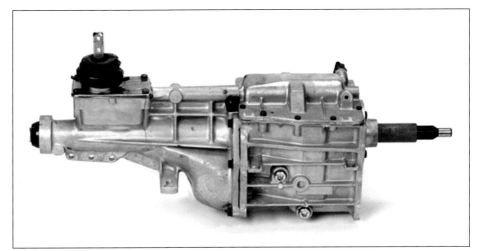

The T-5 World Class 5-speed transmission is standard equipment in the '94-'95 Cobra.

T-45 and T-3650 5-Speeds

The T-45 transmission was used on the 4.6L V-8 powered Mustangs from 1996-2000. An upgraded version, called the T-3650, was released in mid 2000 and used through the 2004 model year. The Mustang changed in 1999 from a mechanical to an electronic speedometer output. Keep this in mind if you're planning a gear swap.

The early T-45 transmissions were not noted for their reliability, especially behind the Cobra engine. Although the stock 2-valve engines were not too hard on the T-45, they started breaking once the owners started adding superchargers and nitrous. As usual, some owners can

A broken or cracked shift 3-4 shift fork is not uncommon in T-45 transmissions that have been drag raced. The OEM shifter has no positive stop, so the fork flexes during power shifts.

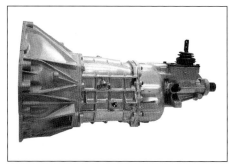

The T-45 5-speed has been used in the 4.6L Mustang GT and Cobra from 1996 until mid 2001, when it was replaced by the T-3650.

get more life from their transmissions than others. I have a couple of clients with 500+ hp cars and after five or six years, they still have the original transmission, while others are on their third or fourth transmission. Honestly, some people could break a hammer in a sandbox!

My favorite manual transmission story involves John Mihovetz, the fastest 4.6L drag racer for a number of years now. Some time ago, he was driving a Mustang with a Doug Nash 5-speed trans in it. While launching the car at a drag race, the driveshaft broke, and tore up the extension housing on the transmission where the shifter bolts on. It broke

with such force, that the shifter, with John's hand still holding on firmly, was forced upward at great speed. It hit the roof of the car, nicely denting the sheetmetal on the outside of the roof. Try explaining that one to the owner of the car! Anyway, after a couple of interim upgrades over the years, Ford replaced the T-45 with a T-3650 in mid-2000 model year. These transmissions were indeed more robust than the T-45, but it is still possible to hurt them with hard shifting and an abundance of torque.

T-56 6-Speed

The 2000 Cobra R, with its torquey 5.4L engine, was released with a T-56 6-speed transmission. The car didn't particularly require six forward speeds, but the increased 440 ft-lb torque capacity of the T-56 gave reliability to what was essentially a factory-produced racecar.

Ford turned to the T-56 again in 2003 for the supercharged Cobra, which required a robust transmission to cope with the power of the supercharged engine. Unlike the 2000 Cobra R version, the '03-'04 Cobra 6-speed had different gear ratios and a smaller output shaft, instead of the 28-spline output of the Cobra R's T-56. However, it did come with a 10-spline input shaft, which has proved to be the Achilles heel of the T-56. Many high-output Cobras have

Aftermarket T-56 six-speed transmissions are popular upgrades with Mustang enthusiasts. More is required to install one of these than just the transmission, however.

simply twisted the input shaft off from too much torque. We first saw this phenomenon in road-race cars in 1999 with the T-45 5-speed trans. We had not seen this before, even on drag cars with slicks. Seemingly, the on-off action of the road-racecars eventually stressed the input shaft back and forth, causing the shaft to fail. Today, 26-spline input shafts are available from G-Force, and Don Walsh from D&D makes some high-capacity T-56 boxes from Viper cores, customizing them for the 4.6L. Dog-face gear engagement is also now available for the T-56 from G-force, and if you have the money, you can even get a full sequential T-56 from Quaife in England.

Aftermarket Transmissions

Let's say you want a stronger manual transmission, but you don't want to rebuild your stock unit. Well, Tremec has some aftermarket 5- and 6-speed transmissions for those Mustang owners wanting to upgrade.

Tremec's latest offerings are the TKO 500 and TKO 600. The two different designations, 500 and 600, refer to the transmissions' torque capacity, 500 or 600 ft-lbs, respectively. The 600 is available in either a wide-ratio setup, with a .64:1 overdrive ratio, or a .82:1 overdrive close-ratio box, which is better suited to road racing. Both are based on the previous TR3550 TKO, a heavy-duty 5-speed that previously was, well, a bit agricultural actually. The new version, however, is a vast improvement, having improved synchronizers and better shift quality. The TKO-600 come with a 26-spline input shaft, which requires a new clutch disc, but that's not too much bother. The 500 and 600 also come with both electronic and mechanical speedometer outputs, covering all years of SN95 Mustangs with one application.

You can get an aluminum bellhousing from Tremec for all of these transmissions to fit a 5.0L, 5.8L, or the 4.6/5.4L. Lakewood makes high-strength steel scat-

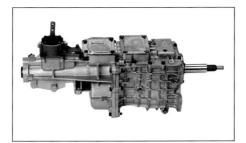

The Tremec TKO 500 aftermarket 5-speed transmission is rated with a 500-ft-lbs torque capacity. A 26-spline input shaft version is also available, the TKO 600, which comes with 600-ft-lb torque capacity.

ter shields, which are required by NHRA for drag racing. Steeda, Hurst, and others make upgraded shifters to fit the Tremec TKO transmissions, too. Tremec recommends either Dexron ATF transmission fluid or a GM synchromesh fluid. We have always felt that the synchromesh fluid performed better in the TKO, especially for motorsport activities.

In addition to the 5-speed transmission, Tremec also offers three aftermarket 6-speed transmissions designed to upgrade '94-2004 Mustangs. One fits the '94-'95 5.0L car, and the other two are for the '96-'98 4.6L and the '99-2004 4.6L, respectively, the difference being a mechanical or electronic speedometer output. The 6-speeds require some additional components for installation, like a shortened driveshaft, transmission mount, reverse solenoid wiring, etc. Installation kits are available from Sean Hyland Motorsport and D&D.

Shifters

The OEM shifter used in the Mustang can really benefit from an upgrade. Billet shifters from Hurst, Pro 5.0, and Steeda offer improved shift quality, shorter throws, and perhaps most importantly, adjustable external stops. These stops keep the internal shift forks from getting bent or cracked with a hard shift. A good shifter is usually among the first upgrades a Mustang owner makes.

A short shifter like this billet Steeda Triax provides shorter, more positive shifts. The adjustable positive stops prevent hard shifting from bending or cracking the transmission shift forks.

Clutch and Flywheel

The clutch assembly is easily the most abused piece of equipment in a performance Mustang, but it's necessary for getting your power to the ground. The '94-'95 5.0L, '96-'98 Cobras, and '96-'99 GT all used a 10.5-inch clutch assembly. In 1999, the Cobra switched up to an 11-inch clutch. The GT got the 11-inch upgrade in 2001, along with the T-3650 5-speed. The factory clutch assemblies are actually quite robust, easily accepting 100 additional horsepower, if not more, without undue failures. Once the clutch needs to be replaced, several reasonably priced choices are available.

This Lakewood scattershield is a hydroformed one-piece bellhousing constructed of high-strength steel. It is designed to contain fragments in case of clutch/flywheel explosion.

Transmission Gear Ratio Chart

Model	1st	2nd	3rd	4th	5th	6th
T-5 (3.8L V-6)	3.35	1.93	1.29	1	0.72	–
T-5 (World Class)	3.35	1.99	1.33	1	0.68	–
T-45	3.37	1.99	1.33	1	0.67	–
T-3560	3.38	2	1.32	1	0.67	–
T-56 (2000 Cobra R)	2.97	2.07	1.43	1	0.8	0.62
T-56 (2003-'04 Cobra)	2.66	1.78	1.3	1	0.8	0.63
T-56 (Aftermarket)	2.97	2.07	1.43	1	0.8	0.62
TKO 500	3.27	1.97	1.34	1	0.68	–
TKO 600 (Close Ratio)	2.92	1.89	1.28	1	0.82	–
TKO 600 (Wide Ratio)	2.92	1.89	1.28	1	0.64	–

All ratios are :1

The M-7560-A302 clutch assembly from Ford Racing is a good choice for a replacement 10.5-inch clutch assembly. It works well on cars up to 450 hp, has performed well for us on road-race cars, and it's only a couple of hundred dollars.

The 2003 Cobra clutch is another really good clutch assembly. It's only available as a flywheel and clutch package. The aluminum flywheel included with the kit provides a substantial reduction in rotating mass, and the clutch, although requiring substantial pedal effort, is up to the task of 600 hp in a street car. You get all this for less than $600 complete. The flywheel is an eight-bolt design, so it only fits Cobra or eight-bolt Windsor cranks used in 2000 GTs. If you have a

Ford's 2003 Cobra aluminum flywheel and 11-inch HD clutch assembly is a great upgrade for any 8-bolt 4.6L application.

The Exedy twin-disc clutch and flywheel combo is rated at over 900 ft-lbs torque capacity. The lightweight billet steel flywheel and forged aluminum cover combined with two clutch discs make this unit very durable on high-horsepower cars, yet docile enough to be used on an everyday street car.

The stock plastic self-adjusting clutch quadrant is known to fail under extreme use, so billet aluminum replacements are available from the aftermarket.

really high-horsepower (say 700 to 1000) Mustang, the best is a dual-disc clutch, like those from Exedy. The dual discs create more surface area to dissipate the heat than a single large disc. The rotating mass is reduced, and the pedal effort can remain reasonable, while still generating a high clamp load to prevent the clutch from slipping.

The Exedy dual-disc clutch features a billet-steel flywheel, billet-aluminum pressure plate, and is available in both 10- or 26-spline hub, but why would you ever use a 10-spline if you had that much power? The dual disc is surprisingly quiet on the street, with virtually no disc rattle when the clutch is disengaged, unlike some earlier versions from other suppliers. At almost $1,700, it is expensive, but if you can afford that much power, you can also afford the clutch to go behind it. If you're planning on drag racing, the stock cast-iron flywheel in your Mustang must be changed up to an SFI-approved billet-steel or billet-aluminum flywheel to be legal. Billet flywheels for both 10.5- and 11-inch clutches are available from Ford Racing and Hays.

Along with the clutch, other upgrades are in order, too. The stock

plastic clutch quadrant has been a weak link in the clutch actuation system since the Fox-body days.

Fortunately, Steeda and others have produced billet quadrants that won't break under the strain of heavy use. Since the adjustment mechanism is deleted with the new quadrant, an adjustable clutch cable is now required to adjust the release point. Recently, firewall adjusters have made the scene too, being easier to adjust on the fly, rather than going under the car.

Automatic Transmissions

The different electronic overdrive automatic transmissions used in '94-2004 Mustangs are all related to each other. The 4R70W was an upgraded version of the AODE transmission, and the 4R75W is a higher-capacity version of the 4R70W trans.

All of the upgrades to these transmissions are similar in nature. Only the specific part numbers vary for each transmission. The usual first modification to an automatic transmission car is a higher-stall torque converter. A typical street car with some 3.73:1 or 4.10:1 rear gears and some bolt-on performance parts,

A firewall clutch disc adjuster provides a convenient method of adjusting the clutch pedal free play.

maybe even a camshaft or four in the case of the Mach 1, can benefit from an increased stall speed in the torque converter. Most stock converters have a stall speed of around 1,800 rpm. Most street performance converters operate in the 2,400- to 3,200-rpm stall speed range, depending on modifications and driver preference. Having a higher stall speed allows the engine to get into the power-producing rev range quicker, and of course, it helps you launch harder from a higher RPM.

Next up is a shift kit, or a complete valve body. One of the cool aspects of the electronically controlled 4R70W/4R75W transmissions is that we can adjust the shift points in drive, the duration of the shift, even the line pressure, using a chip or program downloaded to the engine manage-

A stall converter is one of the best investments for your automatic-equipped Mustang. A small increase in stall RPM can make a dramatic improvement to acceleration.

The 4R75W electronic overdrive transmission used on the '03-'04 Mach 1 is the strongest version used in any of the SN95 Mustangs.

ment computer. In the old days, we had to rely on changing springs and valves in the valve body to make a change in shift quality or RPM. However, we do reach a point where the valve body cannot transfer fluid quickly enough due to its physical limitations. At this point, you need a modified valve body with larger fluid passages, modified accumulator pistons, and the like. The amount of time required to complete a shift – from the time the command is given until the transmission has executed the shift – drops noticeably as a direct result of enhanced fluid flow.

You might also look into a shifter that is better for performance driving. Without a doubt, my favorite is the B&M Megashifter. This ratchet-action shifter pulls only one gear at a time and comes with a Mustang-specific installation kit that looks factory. It's a really nice piece. It also works on the electronic overdrive transmissions or the C4 trans, if you end up switching later on.

The AODE, 4R70W, and 4R75W can be beefed up internally to handle 600 to 700 hp. Heavy-duty planetary gear sets, shaft assemblies, clutches, and bands are available to reinforce these units considerably. Trans brakes are another option available as well. For

The transbrake built into this valve body allows the driver to lock the transmission in both first and reverse gears at the same time, and then electrically release the reverse gear, allowing the car to explode forward off the starting line.

those of you unfamiliar with trans brakes, the reverse and forward gears are locked against each other at the starting line, allowing the converter to flash to peak stall speed. When the light goes green, you release the button, disengaging the reverse gear, allowing the car to launch right now. Usually, transbrakes are found on drag cars, but they are only used for launch, so they are quite streetable.

Changing a 4.6L-powered Mustang over to an automatic is a rewarding change for a car primarily used for drag racing. We have converted a number of cars from manuals to automatics, and with no other changes but a high-stall torque converter we usually see a .4 to .5 second ET reduction. An 11-second-flat Cobra with a 5-speed manual instantly runs 10.50s with a C4 trans, trans brake, and a 5,500-rpm stall converter. The

This '96 Cobra has a B&M Megashifter but it looks factory with the optional trim plate. Of course, the roll cage gives it away that this car has been modified.

torque converter, if properly matched to the engine's power characteristics, keeps the engine operating in a narrow RPM band, right in the peak power part of the curve. This is the reason we get such an ET improvement, particularly with the 4.6L, which does not produce a lot of torque low in the RPM curve. The C4 3-speed transmission is an excellent choice for a car that does not require an overdrive. Properly prepared, the C4 is quite capable of transmitting 850 hp on a reliable basis. Performance Automatic and Dynamic are two of the larger names in the performance C4 trans market. SFI-approved bellhousings and flexplates are available for both the 5.0L and 4.6L engines, and they are required by NHRA for sanctioned drag racing.

One of the keys to longevity with an automatic transmission is to have an adequate transmission cooler. The stock radiator-based trans cooler is not up to the task of cooling a high-performance transmission with a stall converter. Large-capacity trans coolers are usually rated in pounds for towing, so something like an 18,000-lb cooler or better is the ticket. These mount in front of the radiator and should be connected to the

transmission with large diameter 3/8-inch steel lines. The large lines allow a lot of flow when necessary. Trans brakes generate incredible heat while engaged. A temperature increase of 100 degrees per second is possible with the trans brake engaged on a high-horsepower car. For that reason, I only recommend using a trans brake for a maximum of three seconds due to of the temperature rise.

Transmission Mounts

Stock rubber transmission mounts have too much flex for high-performance requirements. While not all Mustang mounts are presently available, the urethane replacement mounts from Energy Suspension or Prothane for manual and automatic transmissions are a sensible upgrade.

Speedometer Calibration

Sooner or later, you may need to calibrate the speedometer for a new transmission, a gear change, or a tire-size change. Mustangs built between '94 and '98 use a mechanical speedo output from the transmission. A selection of drive and

driven gears that allow you to correct for your speedo are available through your Ford dealer.

From 1999 on, it gets even easier, with electronic outputs from the transmissions replacing the old mechanical style. Ford Racing has electronic speedometer calibrators that plug inline to the output from the transmission. The adjustment allows custom calibration for any axle-ratio/tire-size combo, greatly simplifying the process.

A supplementary transmission cooler extends the life of an automatic transmission significantly through reducing the operating temperature.

A C-4 racing automatic transmission can withstand a 900-hp 5.0L or Modular V-8 powerplant.

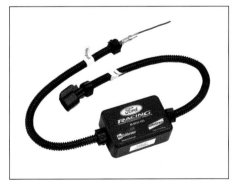

Ford Racing's electronic speedometer calibrator adjusts for axle ratio changes and different tire sizes.

Rear Axles

The '94-2004 Mustang came with three main rear axle variants. All the V-6 cars had a 7.5-inch ring-gear solid axle, one width of housing from '94-'98, and then a wider track from '99-2004. The '94-'98 Mustang GT and Cobra had the 8.8-inch ring gear solid axle, while the '99-2004 Mustang GT and Mach 1 had a wider track version of the same solid axle. Of course, the '99-2004 Cobras had an independent rear suspension that was still based on the 8.8-inch ring-gear size. The many upgrade options for the rear axle assembly based on the type of expected use are discussed here. The 7.5-inch rear has fewer options and is not as strong an axle assembly as the 8.8, so if your V-6 car is going to be used for serious racing activities, or if you just want a wider range of options available to you, swap out the 7.5 for an 8.8. They're inexpensive enough and widely

Ford Racing offers a great selection of ring and pinion gear sets for the 8.8- and 7.5-inch rear ends. Make sure you get your gears installed correctly, or they are noisy.

available both new and used to make this a logical alternative.

Axle Ratios

I get asked several times each week, "What gear ratio should I put in my Mustang?" There is no single answer for this question, but I have my preferences. Many factors that should play into your gear choice: the type of use the car receives, whether or not it's a daily driver, whether or not fuel mileage is a concern, whether long distance drives are part of the car's requirements, etc.

Most Mustangs came from the factory with 3.08:1 or 3.27:1 from '94-'98 and 3.27:1 or 3.55:1 from '99-2004. These ratios are mandated in most cases by CAFE regulations and NVH (noise, vibration, and harshness) concerns – not for optimum performance. Believe me, if the Ford engineers could give us all 3.73:1 and meet their other objectives, they would.

An everyday Mustang used for a variety of activities works well with 3.73:1 gears and still gets decent fuel economy. The improvement in acceleration is noticeable, and yet the engine RPM on the highway is still quite reasonable. This is true for V-6, 5.0L, or 2-valve 4.6L engines. The '96-2001 Cobra and the '03-'04 Mach 1 can benefit even more from a 4.10:1 ratio

because of the extra 1,000 rpm available in the 4-valve engine's operating range. Also, since the 4-valve engine does not produce as much torque in the 2,000 to 3,000-rpm range, the higher ratio gets the engine into its power band more quickly. I wouldn't hesitate to run more gear on a daily driver car that does not need to run down the highway at 70 mph all day. A set of 4.30:1 or even a 4.56:1 is not out of the question on a modified Mustang that makes power in the 4,000 to 7,000 rpm range.

As far as the dragstrip goes, a 4.10:1 ratio combined with a 28-inch tall tire is a popular combination, allowing a trap speed up to about 130 mph at 7,000 rpm. Combinations with higher RPM or mph potential may require a different ratio. The objective is to reach peak operating RPM in high gear just as you pass through the timing lights, so the tire size, power output, and RPM limit all play a role in choosing the best gearing. In road racing,

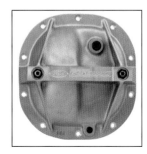

The axle girdle provides additional support to the differential bearing caps, which can prevent breakage, particularly on drag cars, with their extreme shock loads.

Gear Installation Tips

Here is an illustrated installation guide detailing the process of installing a new ring-and-pinion and differential in an 8.8-inch axle assembly. Here are some tips to ensure you have a trouble free life with your new gears and differential.

1. First thing we do is deburr the ring and pinion gear teeth using a die grinder cartridge.

2. The hand model is illustrating the method of hand filing the ring gear mounting surface to ensure that any high spots have been removed.

3. We trial fit the same pinion shim that was originally used in the axle assembly, using special oversize inner-diameter pinion bearings.

4. After trial assembling the pinion and torquing the ring gear to the carrier with new bolts, the ring gear backlash is checked with a dial indicator: .006 to .012 inch is the range – we shoot for .008 inch.

5. The final step in the checking process is to verify the gear tooth contact pattern using gear marking compound. Most of the tooth surface should be in contact and the pattern should be centered in the tooth.

it's a similar deal. You need to gear the car for the maximum speed required on the fastest section of the track. Assuming that your Mustang has a close-ratio fifth gear, a 3.73:1, 4.10:1, or 4.30:1 ratio should be in the ballpark depending on the track.

When installing a new ring and pinion, or a new differential, it's convenient to purchase a complete installation kit like this Ford Racing package.

Once you've selected your gears, you have some other components to consider before you get to the installation. A word on purchasing ring and pinions: Buy them from Ford Racing. Period. The Ford ring and pinions are made on the same equipment as their production gears, so they're dimensionally the same as the stock gears. This means less trouble for you installing them because most of the time the original pinion bearing shim can be reused and is correct for backlash and gear pattern. Whenever someone brings us another brand to install, it inevitably takes longer and is more difficult to install. Just buy the Ford gears – they save you time and money in the long run.

Differentials

Most performance SN95 Mustangs come with Ford's Traction-Lok limited-slip differential. It's adequate for moderate performance use, but it has a low breakaway torque, limiting the amount of power that can be applied to both wheels at the same time. Ford actually supplies an additive for their limited-slip differential that allows smooth slippage between

the friction discs and the steel plates, since most customers are annoyed by differential chatter while cornering in the city. A dyed-in-the-wool enthusiast trades some degree of noise for the ability to put power to the ground through both rear tires.

We can increase the friction in the Traction-Lok by modifying the clutch pack. I first learned to do this back in 1990, when we had to run the original equipment differential in my Firehawk road-race Mustang. Breakaway torque is the amount of torque that can be applied to one wheel while the other is held stationary, before the wheel breaks free. This can actually be measured with a torque wrench and some suitable adapters. A new stock Traction-Lok is in the 80- to 100-ft-lb range. The factory service manual describes a breakaway torque of 20 ft-lbs as an acceptable service limit for an 8.8-inch Traction-Lok differential. You might as well not even have a limited slip differential at that level! The standard Trac-Lok's clutch pack arrangement has alternating friction plates and steel plates. Each side of the differential has three clutch plates and four steel plates. We can add one more friction plate on each side between the two steel plates that come back to back from the factory. This

The Ford Traction-Lok limited slip differential uses friction plates to limit wheel spin. Rebuild kits can renew the differential back to original performance.

increases the friction surface area, and also increases the preload on the "S" spring between the two halves of the differential. We need to be careful we can still get the axle C-clips in, but as long as we can accomplish, this the axle breakaway torque is increased to over 300 ft-lbs. Now the differential has the ability to transfer a much higher level of power before spinning the lightly loaded inside tire.

Eaton makes another plate-type limited-slip differential. The Eaton unit

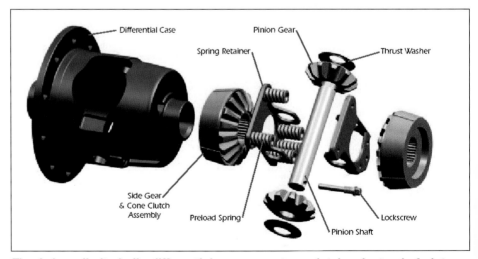

The Auburn limited-slip differential uses cone-type clutches instead of plates. The spring preload between the two opposing friction cones determines the breakaway torque value. (Photo courtesy Auburn Gear)

Auburn ECTED differential has both a cone-type limited slip and an electromagnet that locks the differential solid – making it effectively a spool.

has carbon fiber friction plates, which can operate at much higher temperatures without the differential losing effectiveness. Ford also started using carbon fiber friction material in the Traction-Lok differentials beginning with the 2003 Cobra.

Auburn makes a cone-type limited-slip differential. The Auburn unit uses two cones faced with friction material preloaded against each other with a group of five springs. The two versions of the Auburn are the standard and the Pro series. The Pro series has a higher breakaway torque than the standard, making it a better choice for drag racing and serious open-track racing. The Auburn differential was also used in the 1LE Camaro in the early 1990s, and GM provided a service kit at the time that included competition-level springs and clutch cones to service the differentials. When new, the breakaway torque would be 250 ft-lbs, and they would get rebuilt when the breakaway torque dropped below 150 ft-lbs. The winning teams rebuilt the differential every weekend, just as we did on the Mustang.

Recently, Auburn released an electronic differential (ECTED) that incorporates both a friction cone limited-slip, but when you flip the switch, an

electromagnet locks the differential solid, allowing zero slip between the axles. This is the best of both worlds for a dual-purpose street/racecar. I recently tested an ECTED in a Mustang buildup and I was impressed. It's a really good solution for a street/strip car.

Moving on, other differentials on the market that do not rely on friction materials are available. These are less sensitive to changes due to wear. The Torsen differential uses helical gearing to perform differentiation and torque distribution. The Torsen works as an open differential until one wheel starts to lose traction, and then the difference in torque causes the gears in the differential to bind together. The differential has a torque bias created through the design of the gears, which allows more torque to be applied to the wheel with better traction. The torque bias on the T2 Torsen is 2:1. The T2-R Torsen has the addition of steel clutch plates on the sides with spring preload, for a torque bias of 3.5:1. During acceleration through a turn, weight shifts to the outside wheel, and the inside wheel no longer has enough traction to support the torque load. The Torsen differential transfers torque to the outside wheel before the inside wheel has a chance to slip. Assuming the inside wheel begins to slip at 500 ft-lbs torque input, an open differential with a 1:1 torque bias only applies the same 500 ft-lbs of torque to the outside

wheel before the inside wheel begins spinning. The Torsen T2R with a 3.5:1 torque bias would allow 1750 ft-lbs of torque to be applied to the outer wheel before the inside wheel begins to spin. By comparison, a clutch-type limited slip normally has about a 2:1 torque bias from the factory. The Torsen is a good choice for an open-track or street car where you want a high level of traction with virtually noiseless operation. It's probably not the best choice for a drag car with sticky tires, as high shock loads may inflict wear or damage over time to this type of differential.

The Detroit Locker is an icon for American muscle cars, so of course, it's available for the 8.8-inch Mustang differential. The Detroit Locker is noisy on the street because it functions like the ratchet in your toolbox. Power is applied equally to both wheels when accelerating, but it ratchets as an open differential when you're coasting or decelerating. The locker is a favorite of endurance racers because of its durability, and it's also quite suitable for drag racing.

Both the Torsen and the Detroit Locker offer less influence on a road-racecar's cornering than a friction clutch type limited slip differential. When you are turning in on corner entry, the breakaway torque inherent in a friction limited slip is going to resist differentiating, creating a push or understeer condition

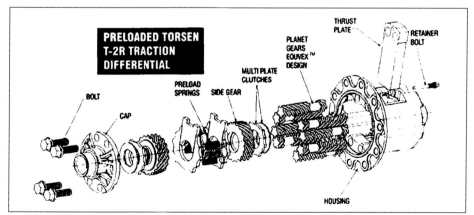

Torsen differentials use helical gearing to provide differentiation and torque distribution. The T-2R Torsen adds steel clutch plates with preload springs to increase the torque bias. (Photo courtesy Torsen)

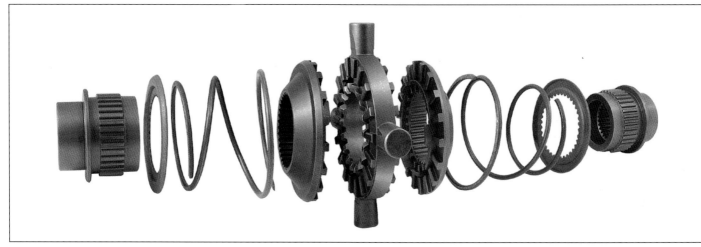

The Detroit Locker uses a mechanical ratchet action to lock wheels together under load and release them while coasting. (Photo courtesy Tractech)

C-Clip eliminators positively retain the axle with a pressed-on bearing and a retaining ring, housed in a billet aluminum carrier.

A spool is the best solution for drag racing, permanently locking the two axles together.

during the corner entry phase. Once the power is applied, the car has a slight power oversteer during corner exit. This is not all bad, mind you, because the corner-entry understeer allows the driver to feel the edge of traction with the front tires. The corner-exit oversteer is controllable with throttle modulation and steering inputs, but this does cost some cornering speed. The Detroit locker is neutral during the corner-entry phase, allowing full differentiation of the rear tires, but the transition to the throttle during corner exit can be ticklish. The transition to fully locked rear wheels under power is sudden and requires smooth driver inputs to avoid sudden changes in the car's attitude.

Every sort of differential has trade-offs, and each may require chassis adjustments to exploit the full potential. Driving style also suits some differentials more than others, so some experimentation may be in order. Real gains can be made by effectively transmitting the power to the tires, so long as you don't exceed the available level of grip.

It gets much easier with pure drag cars. A spool is a mechanical connection joining the two rear axle shafts and eliminating the differential action. This also removes some additional weight from the rotating assembly, freeing up some horsepower to the wheels. A spool is ideal for drag racing, but not too useful on street cars. It is possible to use a spool on the street, but it's not recommended, as the car resists turning corners. Spools are never used in road racecars; well almost never – it's true that one of the most famous road-racecars ever built, the Porsche 917, used a spool. In the 1970s, it was the only solution deemed strong enough for the 1,000-hp sports racer! I haven't heard of anyone using one in a road race Mustang just yet.

When you install a spool on a Mustang 8.8-inch axle, C-clip eliminators must be installed at the same time. Normally, the axle is retained in the axle housing with a C-clip on the end of the axle inside the differential itself. With a spool replacing the differential, there is no method of retaining the axle shaft using a C-clip, so a C-clip eliminator is used. An outer axle bearing is pressed on the axle shaft and retained with a lock ring that is shrunk fit on the axle shaft. The bearing assembly is restrained inside an aluminum enclosure, bolted to the axle flange. This positive retention method also prevents a C-clip or an axle from failing and the car losing an axle shaft at speed on the dragstrip. The NHRA requires C-clip eliminators for the 8.8-inch axle on any car quicker than 10.99 seconds. C-clip eliminators are prone to leaking oil from the axle seal if used on the street or around corners to any extent. They are not recommended for open-track/road-racecars for this reason.

Even with the power outputs of late-model Mustangs regularly exceeding 600 to 700 hp on the street, and over 1,400 hp at the drag strip, we really don't see many differential failures these days. We do, however, see component failure of another highly stressed component. See below.

Axle Shafts

SN95 solid-axle Mustangs came with 28-spline axles shafts from the factory. The '99 Cobra IRS also had 28 splines, while the '01-'04 Cobra came equipped with 31-spline axles.

The stock 28-spline axles are fragile if used with sticky tires. Even a stock Cobra with drag radials can break a 28-spline axle. Increasing the spline count to 31 increases the strength of the axle by

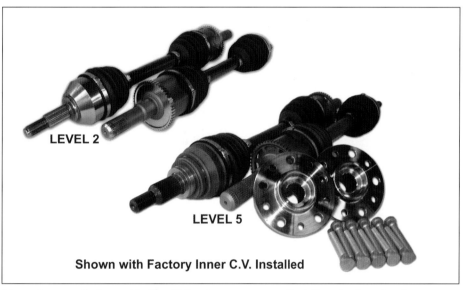

LEVEL 2

LEVEL 5

Shown with Factory Inner C.V. Installed

If you have a Cobra with the IRS setup, you may find the stock axles leave something to be desired in terms of durability. In that case, you can step up to some stronger aftermarket axles. (Photo courtesy The Driveshaft Shop)

Heavy-duty 31-spline axles from Superior Axle have rolled splines for strength, and are forged of alloy steel for improved durability. (Photo courtesy Superior Axle)

some 35 percent. Adding to this, aftermarket alloy axles are built of high-strength alloy steel, which makes them even stronger. Most often, an axle fails at the root of the splines, which is the area of highest stress. It's a really good idea to upgrade the axles at the same time as the differential and/or the ring and pinion are installed. 31-spline aftermarket axles are sufficient for most applications, but if you're running a high-horsepower drag car, 35- and even 40-spline alloy axles are available from specialty axle manufacturers such as Mark Williams and Strange Engineering.

The '03-'04 Cobras, even with their factory 31-spline axles, begin having problems as soon as their owners start adding more power. The splines are strong enough, but the axles themselves are prone to breaking the CV joint when drag raced with slicks. The shock loads are sufficient to crack the cages that contain the CV balls, and then it all goes bad in a hurry. Fortunately, aftermarket axles are available from the Drive Shaft Shop. These 300M axles withstand the shock loads of standing starts and drag slicks much better than the stock axles, and they also offer an outboard CV joint upgrade for the folks who have 900+ hp cars. Most serious drag racers switch out the IRS to a solid axle because it's just so much easier to upgrade the axle components and to tune the suspension.

In case you think road racers are immune to halfshaft problems, we recently had to replace a 28-spline axle shaft that broke on a '99 Cobra open-track car. The car left the track at a great rate of speed, and then rejoined the action on the track. The rear tires were spinning at great speed in the grass and then grabbed the asphalt suddenly upon reaching the track. The axle failed immediately, fracturing inside the differential at the root of the splines. When the IRS Cobras began road racing in 1999, there was a problem with the shaft popping out of the differential. The shaft is retained by a spring clip, and there was insufficient tension to retain the axle shaft under extreme cornering loads. Also, depending on the differential used, the end of the shaft inside the carrier sometimes needs a small amount of material removed in order for the snap ring to fully expand in the groove. The same can be true for the solid axle. Sometimes we find the end of the alloy axle must be dressed to allow the lock pin to slide through the carrier.

Fluid Coolers

We didn't have much problem with the solid-axle cars overheating the differential, but as soon as the IRS arrived in 1999, we sure saw a change. The aluminum case of the IRS expands so much as the temperature rises that the preload on the side bearings goes away, and the next thing you know, you have differential failure. The solution is a good oil cooler for the differential. This is also a dandy idea for high speed Mustangs in open-road races like the Silver State, even with a solid axle. The high speeds encountered in the Silver State, combined with aero management techniques designed to minimize the amount of air traveling under the car, reduce the cooling effect on the axle assembly.

In addition to ducting some air directly toward the differential housing, an external oil cooler, located usually in the trunk, allows the oil to carry some heat away from the differential. I prefer to use a Tilton pump specifically designed for gear oil. The Tilton pump

The differential oil cooler, cooler pump, and lines are visible in the trunk.

Notice the duct, bringing cold air in from the NACA duct on the side quarter window to the differential oil cooler.

passes some trash in the oil without causing the pump to fail, which is important in a long-distance event. A large-capacity cooler core, from Earls or Setrab, is located in the trunk area, and supplied with cool air ducted in from outside the car. Provision must be made to exit the air from the trunk area as well, usually through some vents in the rear panel. A temperature gauge should be installed in the differential housing, allowing the driver the opportunity of monitoring the temperature of the differential oil. The cooler pump should be turned on once the differential oil reaches 150

degrees F. If the driver forgets to turn the differential oil pump on, work over his/her fingers with a small hammer until they remember to do it. Before we started cooling the oil in the IRS housing, the cars would return from a race with the front differential mounting bushings melted from the heat, allowing the housing to clunk back and forth as the power was applied and released by the driver. Simply adding a cooler eliminated the problems.

Speaking of differential temperatures, the oil used in the differential should be tailored to the application.

Different types of differentials require different oils. Auburn recommends 80W90 non-synthetic GL5 gear oil for their limited-slip differential. Auburn and Ford recommend that Ford friction modifier be added to eliminate any chatter during differential operation. You already know my opinion on this, so use it if you must in a street car, but never on a track car. I also recommend a non-synthetic 80W90 gear oil on the Ford Traction-Lok differential. The synthetic oils are just too slippery for the clutch plates or cones, and reduce the breakaway torque. Torsen differentials can use a synthetic or a non-synthetic GL-4 or GL-5 gear oil, according to the manufacturer. I think the Redline heavy shockproof oil would be a good selection, since it contains an extreme pressure additive to cushion gear teeth from shock loads, something I would be concerned with on a Torsen. The Detroit Locker can also be used with either synthetic or regular gear oil, GL-4 or GL-5.

If you have a new ring and pinion in the differential, you should use only non-synthetic gear oil initially. The gears need some time to break in, during which some material is going to be worn from the gear teeth, until all the high spots are worn smooth. A slippery synthetic oil inhibits this process, which is not what we want at all. In fact, a newly assembled differential is going to create a lot of heat during the break in process. Not only are the gears new, and a bit tight against each other, but so are the bearings. The manufacturer's own specifications for the bearing preloads are higher on new bearings than used ones. Virtually no one does this, but the proper break-in procedure for a new ring and pinion is to take the car out, drive it for 10-15 minutes until up to operating temperature, then accelerate and decelerate the car under moderate load several times, return to the shop, and let the differential cool down to ambient temperature before racing it. Once the car has 500 miles on it, or a couple of weekends at the track, drain the oil and refill with new oil of the desired specification. This is cheap insurance, just like an oil change on a fresh engine.

Driveshafts

The standard steel driveshaft works forever and requires low maintenance. But being enthusiasts, we can't just leave well enough alone, can we? A very popular upgrade is the Ford racing aluminum driveshaft. A couple of years ago they were so inexpensive ($180) that I couldn't

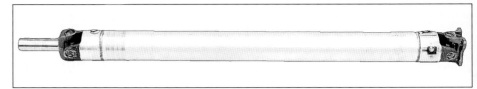

Ford Racing aluminum driveshaft is an excellent lightweight replacement for the stock driveshaft.

A driveshaft safety loop is essential equipment on both drag-race and road-race cars. Certain classes even require them.

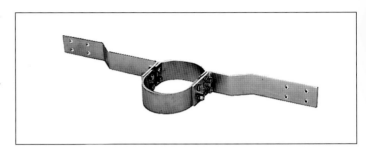

This aluminum spacer is a problem solver when your driveshaft is just a bit too short for your new transmission. Spacers are available in both 3/8-inch and 5/8-inch thicknesses. (Photo Courtesy Steada)

figure out how they could produce them for what they were fetching. Today they have gone up about 40 percent in cost, but they're still a tremendous bargain. The shaft is 14 lbs, half the weight of the stock unit. Reducing the rotating mass frees up a bit of power to the ground. Additionally, the driveline has reduced vibration, especially at really high speeds. The 1999 Cobra in particular had some driveline vibration issues, and an aluminum driveshaft reduces the vibration to an acceptable level.

The Ford Racing driveshaft is stout enough to be used on eight-second drag cars, but you should add a driveshaft safety loop if you are involved in any sort of racing activities. The loop contains the driveshaft in case of a U-joint failure, preventing a nasty accident. Driveshaft loops are required by the NHRA on all cars. Composite driveshafts constructed of carbon fiber bonded to aluminum yokes have become popular in the last few years. They are even lighter than aluminum, and stiffer, resisting twisting to a higher degree. They also offer a potential benefit in case of accident. During a violent crash, composite driveshafts are less likely to bend and pierce the bodywork; they're more likely to break into pieces. For this reason, they are preferred for some races like Silver State, where high-speed crashes can occur. The price on carbon fiber driveshafts has dropped in the past few years as the production methods have improved, and now they are available in the $600 to $700 range. At the end of the day, there is still nothing wrong with a good steel driveshaft, and for many custom applications, we get our local driveshaft shop to make a steel shaft to our requirements, balanced and ready to go.

Aerodynamics

The Mustang had two main shapes between 1994 and 2004, the rounded '94-'98 shape, and of course, the sharp-edged '99-2004 models. Both these schools of design are attractive, and the overall shape of the car is more a function of aesthetics than aerodynamics. The shape was dictated by the desired styling, not a particular aerodynamic value. There are a couple of exceptions, primarily the 2000 Cobra R model. The 2000 Cobra R came from the factory with a high-mounted rear wing and a front splitter. The stock SN95 Mustang generates up to 300 lbs of lift on the front end of the car at 160 mph. The Cobra R aerodynamic parts take car of that.

The Grand Am Cup cars racing at Daytona without any additional aerodynamic aids are so light in the front that at 165 mph, the steering gets pretty light as the front end lifts. The Cobra R was designed as a competition car and spent time in the wind tunnel. Its front splitter eliminates almost all the front-end lift inherent in the stock Mustang. Ford adjusted the overall balance to suit high-speed handling, which usually covers the critical corners of a circuit. The rear wing on the R model is stuck way up in the air, so it has some real effect. The rear wing is really there to balance the effect of the front spoiler. If Ford only added the front splitter, the back end would have been quite twitchy and nervous in some circumstances. The airflow over the roof detaches itself from the rear window as it flows over, meaning the short little factory rear spoiler would not provide any significant downforce. In fact, the rear of the production Mustang actually generates a small amount of lift. By sticking the rear wing up in the air, the airfoil operates in clean air and produces effective downforce. The endplates on the rear wing aren't just there for show either. They prevent air from spilling over the edge of the airfoil, making it effective even when traveling slightly sideways. Overall, Ford did a pretty good job on the Cobra R, adding significant downforce, while only reducing the top speed of the car by five mph with the increased drag of the aerodynamic add-ons.

The 2000 Cobra R incorporates a front splitter and high-mounted rear wing to add downforce while racing. There's a difference between parts engineered for performance, and those designed just for looks.

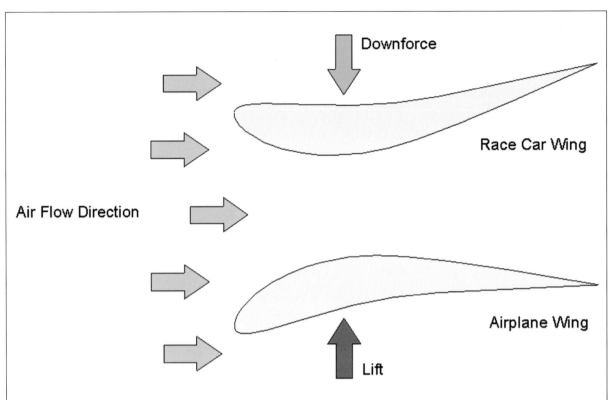

This diagram illustrates how an airplane uses an airfoil to provide lift. Racecars use the same principles, only inverted, to provide downforce.

You can see the aluminum-clad board added on the lower surface of the splitter to add strength and reduce deflection.

Okay, so much for the history lesson, let's talk about what we can do to specifically improve the aerodynamics of our Mustang.

Front Splitters

The objective with any aerodynamic device that we add, front splitter or rear wing, is to add downforce, improving the overall grip of the car without adding more drag than is necessary. The aerodynamic drag of a car is expressed as a coefficient of drag or Cd figure. The Mustang has a Cd of .36. By way of comparison, a C5 Corvette has a Cd of .29, and a Hummer has a Cd of .57! The higher the Cd number, the more power is required to achieve a given speed, all other things being equal. With a front splitter, our objective is to separate the air, limiting the amount of air going under the car, reducing drag and using the airflow over the top of the car to create downforce. To create downforce, we need to shape the front of the spoiler like an airfoil. An airfoil or wing creates lift in the case of an airplane, or downforce in the case of an automobile. It does this by accelerating the speed of the air over one surface, creating a low-pressure area, and maintaining the speed of the air over the opposite surface, creating a high-pressure area. The difference in air pressure at both surfaces creates lift or downforce as the case may be.

The Cobra R-style splitter only fits the '99-2001 Cobra front fascia. Steeda has produced a similar splitter for the '03-'04 Cobra fascia, and another that fits the '99-2004 GT fascia. All of these splitters seem to deflect downward at high speed, reducing the effectiveness of the splitter, and bending the splitter down to the point it can contact the track surface in some cases. We make an additional panel from 1/2-inch-thick aluminum sheet wrapped around plastic honeycomb. This material, which is very light and extremely rigid, is available from sign shops.

By adding a panel to the lower splitter surface and extending it back to the leading edge of the front wheel well, we add a tremendous amount of rigidity to the splitter, increasing its effectiveness. We also add two one-inch-round aluminum bars between the honeycomb panel and the bottom of the bumper reinforcement bar.

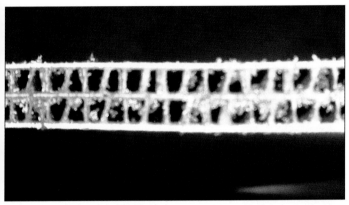

Combining an aluminum sheet exterior with a lightweight plastic core makes for a rigid splitter material.

Aluminum bars attach to the bumper for reinforcement, further adding strength to splitter assembly.

Air ducts placed in the '03-'04 Cobra hood increase radiator efficiency and reduce high-pressure air buildup in engine compartment. This can apply to other hoods too.

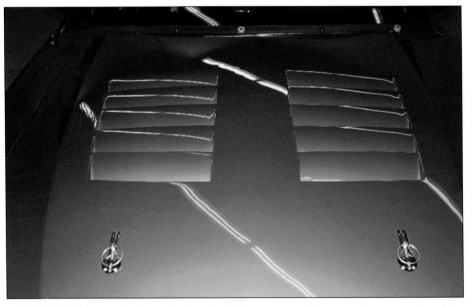

Vents have been added to the hood of this open-track car to improve aerodynamics and efficiency.

This prevents the panel from deflecting, and ties the entire assembly together. If we want to have some adjustability to the front end, we can make up a splitter extension of 3/16-inch T6061 aluminum and slot it, allowing the extension to slide in and out from the leading edge of the splitter. The more area we have on the splitter, the more downforce we make, and the sliding extension allows us to balance the front and rear aero to suit the track.

As with suspension tuning, aero tuning involves compromise, so the correct aero balance for one portion of the track may not be optimum for another. At the end of the day, we optimize for the most important corners and adjust our driving style for the rest.

Those of you with '94-'98 Mustangs are going to have to work a bit harder to find a good front splitter. The Saleen front splitter/valance could work with additional support. Hardcorestangs has a complete replacement fascia and splitter for '94-'98 cars that incorporates a later-model-style splitter. It's hard to get a splitter that looks right on the early rounded-edge cars.

Another modification that reduces front-end lift, although it does not create any downforce on its own per se, is to vent the hood. Air rushing through the radiator and under the front of the car gets trapped in the engine compartment, resulting in front-end lift and lack of airflow through the engine compartment. It's no mistake that Ford installed two vents in the hood of the '03-'04 Cobra.

The vents increased the airflow through the radiator and intercooler heat exchanger over the previous model year, simply by providing an outlet for the air trapped under the hood. Placing the vents in the hood of the '03 Cobra also reduced front-end lift by some 120 lbs.

Adding vents in the hood of your Mustang can have the same effect, improving cooling and enhancing downforce. The positioning of the vents is fairly important. They need to be placed 1/3 to 1/2 way back from the leading edge of the hood to be effective.

If you put them too far back, the air does not flow through past all the obstructions.

Rear Wings

The rear wing needs to be elevated above the trunk lid in order for it to get into some clean air. The rear wing needs to be 8 to 12 inches above the trunk lid in order to be effective. The wing should also be located as far rearward as possible, again taking advantage of as much clean air as possible.

The wing section determines both the amount of downforce and aero drag it creates. Each specific wing section has an L/D ratio that expresses the amount of Lift divided by the amount of Drag. This is the reason you see open wheel CART racecars with several different rear wing configurations. On a short 1-mile oval like Phoenix, they run a high-downforce/high-drag wing, since the car never gets near its top speed anyway. The extra downforce helps them corner at the highest possible speed. On a big 2-1/2-mile oval like Michigan, the cars run a low-downforce/low-drag wing configuration since the top speed approaches 230 mph. A road-course wing setup is somewhere between the two extremes, with a medium downforce/medium drag configuration to effectively provide downforce for cornering and acceptable drag for the straights. Likewise, the front wing is changed or adjusted to balance the specific type of rear wing being used at a given circuit.

Anyone interested in a specific wing profile for a given application would be advised to look into some books on the subject. Theory of Wing Sections by Abbott and Von Doenhoff is one of the best. It contains the L/D ratios of many different wing profiles and an amazing amount of information on wings and airflow.

Supporting a rear wing on the trunk lid is one way to do it; another is to fabricate supports that extend down

Cobra R wing is high enough to catch clean air off the roof, maximizing the efficiency of the wing

into the trunk area and attach to the floor. Wings that generate significant downforce should be mounted directly to the chassis, rather than deflecting the trunk lid at speed. Wings themselves can be fabricated of aluminum sheet, curved over aluminum or plywood patterns, or fiberglass or carbon fiber laid on top of a foam core. The size and shape of the wing endplates also play a role in its performance. When the car is drifting sideways somewhat, the end plates keep the air from

running off the end of the wing, and so, the size and shape of the endplate determines the downforce and drag of the wing under certain conditions. Since most rear wings used on Mustangs are going to be fixed-angle wings, it's difficult to change the amount of downforce once a wing has been selected and installed.

One simple method of increasing the downforce is to add a wickerbill, which is a piece of 1/2-inch aluminum bolted or riveted to the trailing edge of

Adding a wicker bill to the trailing edge of the wing can increase the downforce significantly at the expense of some additional drag.

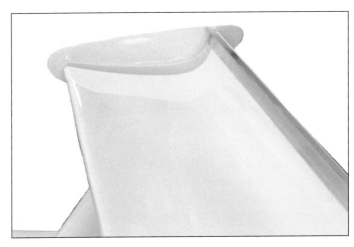

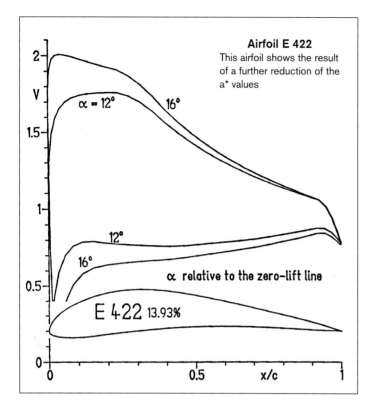

Airfoil E 422
This airfoil shows the result of a further reduction of the a* values

$\alpha = 12°$ 16°

α relative to the zero-lift line

12°
16°

E 422 13.93%

This is the cross section of one type of airfoil. Different airfoil designs offer alternative downforce versus drag coefficients.

the wing. The wickerbill disturbs the exiting air, increasing downforce significantly, but it also adds substantial drag. Nonetheless, it's a simple, effective way of increasing downforce on a track where you do reach terminal speed, but extra downforce could be a benefit.

A word about aftermarket wings. Some wing designs, although pleasing to the eye, do not work well. Even more troubling is the fact that some designs actually cause stability problems. We were doing some work on a 1999 Cobra that had some stability issues on the highway. We checked the alignment, looked for a bad shock, and even tried another set of tires from a different car. This car was truly evil. At only 70 mph, it took all your concentration just to keep the car in its own lane. The car was so twitchy, that it just felt like it would turn around on you at any moment. The car had a unique rear wing, almost like a Porsche whale tail sort of thing, so we removed it just to see. The car was instantly transformed back into a civilized performance car. Therefore, even at relatively low speeds, the effect of poor

design can be a significant problem. If you are purchasing a wing or body kit for its curb appeal, that's fine, nothing wrong with that, just make sure it doesn't create a new set of problems. Since I'm on the subject, most of the aftermarket rear wings made of aluminum that I see have brackets that are so flimsy the wing won't work well at all. You would be further ahead to purchase a wing and brackets from a proper racecar fabricator, or make one yourself, than to use one of those toy wings on the rear of your Mustang.

Drag Cars

Door-slammer Mustang racecars are often seen sporting aluminum rear wings that extend back 14-18 inches past the edge of the trunk lid. I imagine some of you are wondering if they work, since they aren't stuck up in the air. The answer is yes and no. Most drag racing classes do not permit an airfoil to be mounted up in the air, with the exception of Dragsters, Funny Cars, and Pro Mods, all of which have enough power to spin the tires at virtually any speed

without some significant downforce. The rules force door-slammer Mustangs to use only a spoiler attached to the rear of the trunk lid. The spoiler only has air passing on the top surface, not the underside, so no downforce can be created. This is the best they can do within the context of the rules. By extending the surface of the trunk lid into a spoiler, the air traveling over the roof detaches from the rear window but reattaches itself to the flat surface of the spoiler. This reduces drag, freeing up some horsepower. Additionally, there are usually short vertical stabilizers running fore and aft on the spoiler. Sometimes you also see these on the roof surface. These vertical stabilizers, seldom more than an inch high, help keep the car going straight. If the car gets loose and starts to go sideways a bit, the force exerted on the stabilizers helps straighten the car out.

Remember, most of the cars we are speaking of here are running between 180 and 220 mph at the top end, so we're looking at some significant forces acting upon the car at those speeds. The trailing end of the spoiler usually has a slight wickerbill built into the surface as an attempt to gain a little downforce as the air exits the spoiler. As with all aerodynamic aids, small adjustments to the spoiler can make the car easier and more comfortable to drive at speed. Although most Mustang drag cars do not utilize a full front splitter, the leading edge of the really fast cars usually feature a sharp edge to force the air up over the surface of the body and keep it from going underneath. As you can imagine, air getting underneath the front of a drag car at 200 mph can have disastrous consequences. When a car's attitude changes during the course of a run, it has aerodynamic consequences. Electronic adjustable rear shocks have become prevalent on door slammers in the past few years. They allow the driver to change the rear shock valving as the car travels down the track and the aero loads increase. Pretty slick, eh?

The spoiler on the rear of this drag car is not going to create any significant downforce due to the rules of the class. Instead, the objective with the rear spoiler is to extend the deck lid surface, allowing the air passing over the roof to reattach to the spoiler, reducing drag and increasing top speed.

High-Speed Mustangs

Some hardcore Mustang enthusiasts like to participate in high-speed open-road races like the Silver State Classic. These events have classes in different speed ranges (130 mph, 140 mph, etc.), but the big dogs run in the unlimited class. We were involved with a 1997 Cobra that achieved 207 mph top speed in the 2000 race, with an average speed of 187 mph over the 90-mile course. Aero management is important at those speeds, and special techniques are employed. One of the objectives with a top-speed car is to reduce the frontal area, making as small a hole as possible through the air. Removing the side mirrors, windshield wipers, window moldings, and other small details make a difference as to the power required to achieve a given speed. Power required to reach a given speed goes up as a function of the square of the speed. In other words, if you want to double your speed, you need four times the power.

My favorite story about high-speed aero involves an enthusiast who took delivery of a brand new Porsche tuned by a famous German tuning firm. Upon receipt of the car at the airport in New Jersey, the customer took the car to an abandoned airport runway and ran the car up to top speed while a friend tracked him with a radar gun. The top speed was 198 mph. The customer was not happy. He was told the terminal velocity of his new toy would be 201 mph. He immediately got on the phone to Germany and explained the situation to the service manager at the famous German tuning firm. After listening patiently to the customers complaint the service manager utters just four words: "Fold zee mirrors back." Sure enough, upon adjusting the mirrors, he hit 201 mph.

The Mustang I mentioned that ran top speed at Silver State used a skirt made of plastic to fully enclose the lower edge of the car, preventing air from going underneath. The radiator opening was just large enough for cooling and no more. This is so critical to speed that stock cars regularly tape up most of the radiator duct, making the car just a little more aerodynamic for qualifying runs, which only last for three or four laps.

We installed a high-mounted rear wing with low drag relative to downforce to keep the rear of the car from lifting at speed. The owner had done extensive research on aerodynamics and had done as much as possible to minimize the drag. The fact that it only took 550 rwhp to get the car to 207 mph is a testament to the aero management he employed. The limiting factor on the Mustang top speed car was the nose itself, which would have required a significant redesign in order to make a substantial improvement.

Ride Height

From an aerodynamic standpoint, we want to set the car's ride height to give us 1/2 to 1 inch of rake on the body. You can measure this using the rocker panel at the pinch weld. The rake helps generate some downforce on the body shell itself, and more importantly, prevents air from getting trapped underneath the front splitter. If you remember seeing the Mercedes cars doing back flips at Lemans a few years ago – that was an extreme example of air getting under a front splitter, combined with a long splitter length forward of the front wheel centerline.

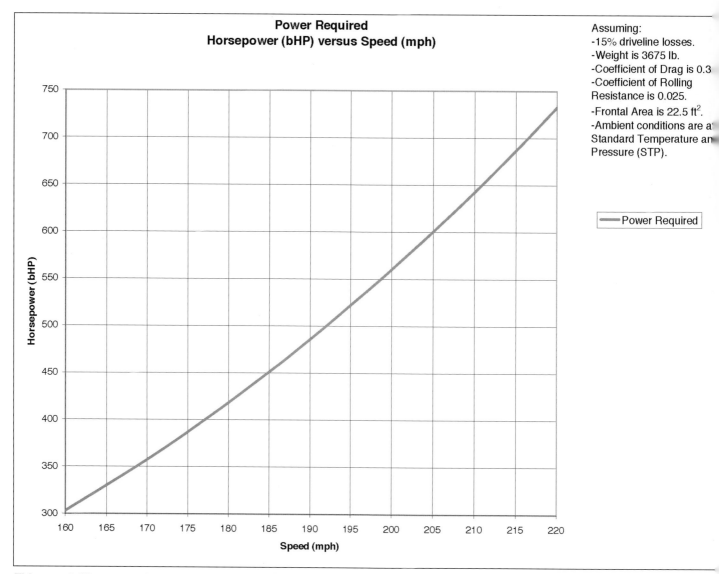

Power Required
Horsepower (bHP) versus Speed (mph)

Assuming:
-15% driveline losses.
-Weight is 3675 lb.
-Coefficient of Drag is 0.3
-Coefficient of Rolling Resistance is 0.025.
-Frontal Area is 22.5 ft².
-Ambient conditions are at Standard Temperature and Pressure (STP).

Power Required

This graph illustrates the huge power increases required as the terminal speed of the car increases.

This made the car pitch sensitive and liftoff occurred when the wrong set of circumstances came together. Aerodynamic suspension deflection is an important consideration at speed as well. Since we usually run a much softer spring rate on the rear, we need to be careful that as the rear downforce increases at speed, it doesn't compress the rear too far, changing the rake angle in a negative way. A simple way to measure this is to place tie wraps around the shock pistons, and measure the movement of the tie wrap after a track session.

When you have a racecar that's going to run at a high-speed track like Daytona, which also causes centrifugal force from its 31-degree banking, the car compresses the springs much more than from the effect of aero alone. Rub blocks made of balsa wood can be attached with racer's tape to the underside of the chassis – two in the front, two at the rear – to determine how close the chassis is coming to the track surface. These can be replaced with permanent rub blocks later, of nylon, or even better, titanium. If you race at night, the shower of sparks tells you when you've bottomed out.

If you want to see if the air is following the path you think it is, there are some low-buck ways to collect information. One is the wool tuft test, where you tape short pieces of yarn four or five inches apart from each other over an entire car, or even just the part of a car you want to study. By using a contrasting color, you can photograph the car at speed and have a clear picture of how the air is flowing over the surface. Another method involves using a viscous liquid like ketchup or vegetable oil, applying a few drops over a surface and then inspecting the direction of movement of the liquid after a high-speed run.

I spoke with George Klass recently about aerodynamics and cars. George knows a great deal on the subject, having worked on Craig Breedlove's land speed record team for several years while the land speed record was hover-

This Mustang has been modified for top-speed runs in the Silver State Classic race. Note the side skirts and front skirt, designed to minimize air passing under the car. Also note the small radiator opening and high mounted rear wing. This car achieved 207 mph during one race.

ing around 600 mph. George has been the technical director for the Fun Ford series for the past several years and he had some interesting comments on the state of aerodynamics and the Mustang racer. He said he is amazed by the number of cars with aero devices not working the way they could be. The pits are full of cars with cowl induction hoods that are too far away from the windshield to benefit from the high-pressure area at the base of the windshield, 180-mph drag cars with side-view mirrors attached, rear spoilers with no side plates to keep the air from spilling off the sides, and hood scoops that do not have air going in them due to placement or design issues. He went on to say that the crews who understand and manage aero on their racecars have stable and predictable cars at high speed. What he didn't have to say was that the teams that manage their aero effectively also win a lot of the races.

Some racers set the ride height with a tape measure off the rocker panel. The front of the car should always be 1/2 to 1 inch lower than the rear to maintain aero balance as the suspension compresses.

Safety Equipment

Seats

Production Mustang seats have several requirements to fulfill. They need to be stylish, durable, adjust to suit a wide range of drivers, and be cost effective to manufacture. This is all well and good, but what exactly does a seat do for the driver? The seat needs to allow the driver to work the pedals, steering wheel, and shifter, while traveling at speed, without sliding all over the place, and/or having to brace his/her self against the door/transmission tunnel/dash with parts of the body in order to stay upright. The stock seats in most Mustangs do not do a good job of locating the driver and providing support while the car is being driven in a sporting manner. The '94-'98 Mustang seats also seem to suffer from early job burnout, the springs in the seat cushion all going catawampus after only three or four years service. The Cobra seats from 1999 onward are actually pretty decent seats, and the foam is more rigid than the '94-'98 seats ever were. Those on a budget might do well to look at some late-model Cobra seats as a worthwhile upgrade to an earlier Mustang.

The later Cobra seats also have suede centers, which provides more grip against your clothing, causing you to slide around far less than on a pure leather seat. Of course, the best produc-

The '99-2004 Cobra seats, with their suede inserts and bolsters, provide the best support of any of the SN95 seats.

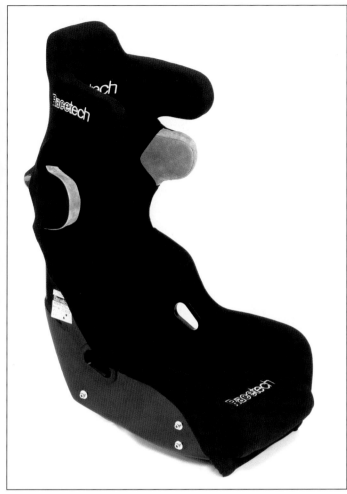

This Racetech racing seat has wrap-around shoulder supports and helmet side supports to keep your head supported while cornering. (Photo courtesy Racetech)

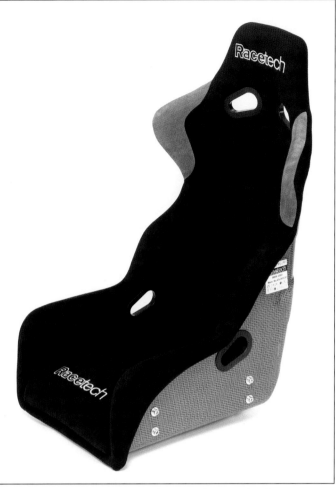

Here's another version of a Racetech seat that's more suitable for a dual-purpose street/open track Mustang. Its bolstering is less extreme, but still much better than a stock seat. (Photo courtesy Racetech)

tion seats in the '94-2004 Mustangs were the Recaro seats found in the Cobra R models, but the chances of scoring a good used Recaro from an R model are about the same as winning the lottery. Aftermarket seats come in all manner of sizes, styles, and price ranges. The trick is to choose a seat that suits your needs, your body, and your pocketbook. First, let's analyze the requirement of the seat, relative to the type of use it's going to see. If we want an all-round kind of seat, something we can use in our daily driver but that also provides us with more support for open-track events, occasional drag racing, and long-distance driving, then a Cobra seat or an entry-level Recaro might be appropriate.

If, on the other hand, you have a street/strip warrior, something you drag race every weekend and seldom drive on the street, then an aluminum Kirkey or plastic Jaz seat might be the ticket. Either of these lightweight seats shaves some pounds off and gets the job done on those short quarter-mile blasts.

A serious open-track or road-race enthusiast is going to want a seat with maximum lateral support to really hold him/her in tight while cornering at over one g. In this case, an OMP, Sparco, or Racetech seat is the order of the day. Each type and where it's best suited are examined here.

OEM seats are most often made of steel stampings or tubular fabrications

covered with foam and an outer covering of leather or cloth. Aftermarket seats are made of several different materials. Many of the Sparco, Recaro, and Cobra seats are made of tubular steel covered with varying densities of foam and a breathable fabric covering. The different densities of foam are used in different areas of the seat according to pressure.

Some areas of a seat have pressure points, like the bottom where your bum sits, the front edge of the seat where your thigh rests on the edge, and the top 1/3 of the seatback, where your shoulders contact. These areas can benefit from increased support underneath while maintaining a comfortable

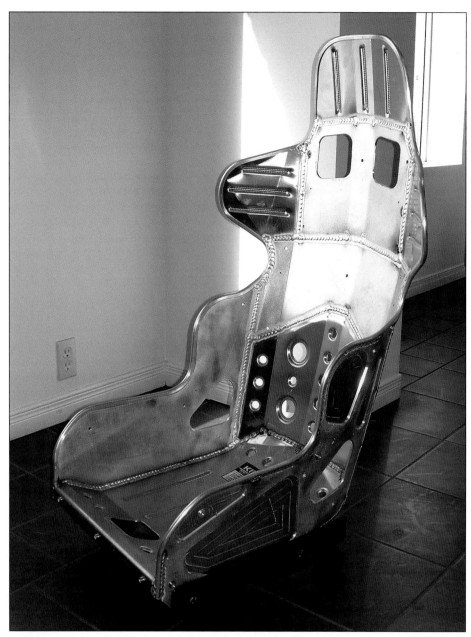

This Kirkey aluminum seat is TIG welded together from many pieces. The seats can be ordered in several widths according to requirements. Note that the seat has been lightened with CNC machining on the side of the seat.

area. Drivers who are taller or shorter, skinnier or larger than average are always going to be more challenged to find the ideal seat. One of the reasons I like driving Mustangs is that the car really fits smaller drivers like me, although drivers much over 6 feet tall have difficulty. Kenny Brown makes a dandy seat bracket extender that allows the stock seat tracks to move an additional four inches rearward. This is ideal for a tall driver to get the legs and arms in the correct relationship with the pedals and steering wheel. Don't be afraid to customize an aftermarket seat to suit your needs. Adding some additional foam in a spot here or there can be done at home or by a local trim shop. I view the purchase of a good seat as a purchase that can be amortized over a long period of time, moving from car to car. Just remember to keep the original seat in a clean, dry storage spot, so it's useable when the day comes to trade up to a newer Mustang.

Drag-Race Seats

Drag-race Mustangs can really benefit from a lightweight seat like a Kirkey aluminum seat. These seats are fabricated from tig-welded 6061-T6 aluminum. The sides are even CNC'd for lighter weight and maximum rigidity. Kirkey seats can be ordered in various widths, and feature snap in covers of fabric or leatherette over a thin layer of foam. These seats are not designed for driving across the country, but they are pretty good for drag racing and even occasional street driving. They come standard with slots for competition 5-point belts, which makes them easier to install as well. Average seat weight on a Kirkey is about 15 lbs, which means a pair of these save you 80 lbs off the weight of the standard Mustang seats. The side of the seats are drilled and tapped, providing an easy place to attach brackets and mount the seat.

The Jaz molded polyethylene (lightweight plastic) seat is another

contact with the body. Using pliable outer foam with denser foam underneath is one method of achieving this. In fact, there may be several densities of foam in some seats. Things that I like to look for in an aftermarket touring type seat like are: good support under my thighs at the edge of the seat, a snug fit at my hips so I'm not going to slide around, and support in the middle of my back.

Since many seats offer extra padding in the shoulder area, sometimes the small of the back is left unsupported, which quickly causes fatigue on a long drive. I also want a fabric that breathes well, because I hate being sticky when it's warm out there. I also want a street seat that has seatback angle adjustment, not a fixed rake, and a latch to allow the seatback to flip forward, allowing access to the rear seat option for a lightweight drag seat. They're available with a snap-in cover, and they have slots for competition belts. These Jaz seats are not as rigid or as strong as the aluminum seats, but as an economical, lightweight seat, it does the job.

Road-Race/Open-Track Seats

Most road-race seats are constructed of fiberglass or carbon fiber, sometimes with Kevlar included in the mix. This provides a lightweight seat with excellent rigidity. Good race seats have an FIA certification on the back of the seat, attesting to the fact that the seat design was tested in accordance with strict FIA standards for performance during an impact and that it passed those tests. OMP, Sparco, Momo, and Recaro are some of the better-known names in race seats. What we are looking for here is a seat with high side bolsters, as getting in and out of the seat easily is no longer important. These seats are available in various widths to suit most body types, so the sides of the seat should grip you snugly at the hips, and the thigh should have good support, yet allow the legs to move quickly and freely across the pedals.

Balancing the car on the edge of control requires dancing the feet across the pedals in a medley of braking, accelerating, downshifting – applying the clutch, accelerator and brake all simultaneously – and the edge of the seat cannot inhibit this motion. The seatback should wrap around your shoulders, providing support to the upper body during substantial cornering loads. The padding should be adequate for comfort, but still allow the chassis to communicate with your derriere. This is after all, your primary feedback when flirting with the edge of the traction circle, and we want it to be a local call, not long distance. I know that everyone out there is thinking, "man this guy is anal about seating position," but I can't overstate how impor-

The Kirkey seat in this track car has a snap-on nylon and foam cover installed.

This is an FIA standard label applied to an OMP carbon Kevlar seat. This seat meets the requirements for racing as set forth by the FIA governing body for motorsport worldwide.

tant it is to be really comfortable and secure to truly drive a car quickly. To that end, when installing seats, be fussy about the height, the distance from the steering wheel, the rake of the seat bottom/back. An extra hour or two to get the seat in exactly the right position for you are well worth the effort. Shims can be made from washers and brackets can be drilled for multiple locations to get the rake perfect. Sometimes, the seat tracks available from the seat manufacturer work. We are fortunate that the Mustang is popular enough that most seat manufacturers have Mustang-specific brackets available. If the available mounts don't fit your needs, fabrication is the order of the day. Sometimes universal seat brackets can be used, but more often we use the stock Mustang seat brackets and modify them to work. Once we have the seating sorted out, we need to look at seat belts.

Seat Belts

The stock three-point lap and shoulder belt hardly provides the restraint we need for spirited driving. While adequate on the highway, once we start tossing the car around on an autocross course or an open track, even drag racing, it becomes inadequate. A simple and effective solution for dual-purpose cars is a device called the CG Lock. This attaches to your stock seat belts, and provides a positive latch across your lap. This means the recoil mechanism won't over tighten, or loosen off, at inappropriate times. It makes the standard belt quite useable for open track or solo activities, and it's quite inexpensive to boot. Also with a CG Lock, you don't need special seats as with competition belts.

Competition restraint systems can have four, five, or six mounting points. The requirements of your race series may dictate the minimum requirements for your situation, but I would consider a three-inch lap belt, three-inch shoulder belts, and a 2-inch crotch strap to be

The CG Lock is installed on the standard front seatbelt, preventing the belt from loosening or tightening while driving in a spirited manner. This is a great solution for part-time open-track cars.

A race belt like this Sabelt five-point harness keeps you snug in your seat.

This roll bar has a bolt-in cross bar to attach the belts to. It's removable when you're not at the track, so it's a great idea in a dual-purpose car.

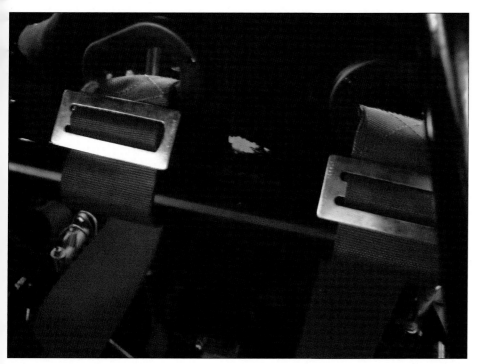

The preferred method of mounting shoulder belts is to loop them around the roll-cage crossbar.

the minimum. These five belts are going to connect together with either an over center latch or a rotating center latch design. Each type has its devotees, but largely it is a matter of personal preference. Some like the over center latch, but I find it too bulky across my midsection.

Some claim that you can visually confirm that all the pieces are latched in place with the over center design, and that sometimes you can miss an improperly latched belt in a rotating center design. Horse puckey I say! It's the driver's responsibility to ensure the belt is latched securely, and a proper latch audibly clicks when the belt end is latched, after which the driver should tug on the belt to confirm that it's secure. In my opinion, Sabelt makes the best competition restraints. Their latch mechanism is superior to most others. Sabelt products are made in Europe and are usually only available in North America by mail order. It's no coincidence that many Formula 1 and World Rally teams use Sabelt. You get what you pay for in most cases, and safety equipment is not the place to go economy. Competition belts come with a tag sewn on that certifies that the belts meet SFI standards and gives the manufacture date. Most sanctioning bodies require belts to be replaced at regular intervals, usually three years from date of manufacture, as exposure to UV light and sweat breaks down the material. In the event that the car is involved in an accident, the belts must be replaced. The fabric in the belts is designed to stretch in the case of an accident, as your body is thrown against them. This built-in cushion effect lessens injuries by reducing your body's rate of deceleration. Once the stretch factor is used up, the belt no longer stretches to reduce injury and must be replaced. Once again, it's the driver's responsibility to make sure this happens. Mounting the competition belts properly is of paramount importance to their performance during a crash. Improperly mounted belts can kill a driver.

In the Mustang, my preference is to use the original mounting points for the lap portion of the belts, using a forged eyehook screwed into the stock mounting lug. The floor is reinforced in this area, and it is easy to use. Failing this –

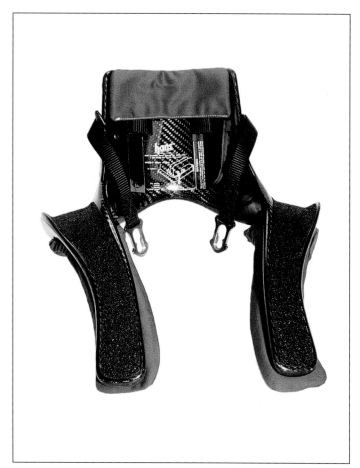

The HANS Device is a helmet restraint system that reduces the whiplash effect on the neck.

or on cars with non-stock floor pans, forged eyebolts with 1/8-inch mild steel back-up plates, a minimum of three inches square – provides adequate reinforcement. Shoulder belts should always be mounted to the roll bar cross tube. Mounting them to the floor creates spinal compression during a crash, causing unnecessary injury. The FIA has specific requirements for the mounting of seat belts, which should be used as a guideline for any form of motorsport. Once the belts are mounted and the seat adjusted, it's just as important to adjust the belts to suit the driver. The lap belt needs to be worn low across the hips, where the pelvis has the most strength. Internal organ injuries are more likely during an accident if the belt rides up above the pelvis. The crotch strap adjustment keeps the lap belts from riding up into the abdomen. This is the major reason a four-point

restraint system should not be used – the lap belt cannot be kept in its proper position. The shoulder belts are adjusted last, and need to be pretty snug. It is often helpful to have someone outside the car cinch down the adjusters on the belts, as the driver doesn't have the angle or the leverage for the lap belt adjustment in particular.

The HANS device is a relatively new piece of safety equipment that is becoming required more and more by sanctioning bodies. The HANS device attaches to the driver's helmet, and the shoulder belts of the restraint system. The device slows down the forward movement of the head and neck during an accident, preventing basal skull fracture, which is fatal. NASCAR drivers Dale Earnhardt and Adam Petty died from just such an injury. Major race series such as NASCAR, Formula 1, IRL, and others now require all driv-

ers competing in their series to use the HANS device or similar product. Even drag racers should seriously look at using the HANS device in any car quicker than 11 seconds. I am old enough to remember when racing was dangerous and sex was safe, and there's no reason why a serious racing accident shouldn't be survivable today, given the advanced equipment at our disposal. The HANS device does require a specific safety harness system, so be sure and look at the requirements at the same time you are shopping for belts.

Helmets

Proper helmets for drag racing, open track, and road racing have a sticker inside from the Snell Foundation. This organization has been designing and administering tests for helmets

A full-face helmet like this Simpson Bandit provides more protection than an open-face helmet.

This Simpson Sidewinder Shark helmet has provision for fresh air to be pumped into the helmet.

since the 1960s. Motorsport helmets have different requirements than motorcycle helmets do, owing to different types of impacts generated by the two different activities. Although Snell tests both types, we want to make sure the helmets we use are the correct type for motorsport activities. A year is listed – 2000, 2005, etc. Most sanctioning bodies have their requirements listed, and you should always purchase the latest specification.

The choice between an open-face and a full-face helmet seems like a no brainer, but some people still haven't figured it out. I used to be an open-faced helmet wearer myself; driving closed-cockpit cars, it didn't seem like I was taking much of a chance. But then I went to some SAE conferences where driver safety was discussed by experts in the field. They cited actual case studies, changing my outlook. I advocate full-face helmets for any motorsport endeavor. The problem is, the body and restraint system stretch so much in a collision, that the body is likely to hit objects inside the car during an acci-

An aftermarket steering wheel like this Momo Commando provides the driver with an excellent surface to grip, contoured to the shape of the driver's hands.

dent, even though these objects may be some distance away. The face, particularly the chin and jaw, are quite capable of hitting the steering wheel or steering column during a collision, and without a full face helmet to protect them, severe, even fatal injuries can occur.

Buy a good-quality helmet, make sure it is the proper size for you, and take care of it, so it can take care of you. If you drop a helmet on a hard floor or pavement surface, it may be damaged, unseen by the eye, but now incapable of providing the proper protection during a collision. In this instance, send the helmet back to the manufacturer and have it inspected. They are the only people qualified to determine if the helmet is still suitable for use or not. Should you be involved in an incident where the helmet sustains an impact, the helmet should be replaced. If the collision is serious enough to require medical attention, the helmet should be sent to the hospital with the driver to provide medical staff useful information on the location and extent of possible head trauma. Simpson and Bell are two of the better-known names in motorsport helmets. Both have a good dealer network, so take the time to try them on and get the right one for you.

Steering Wheel

Changing the factory steering wheel for an aftermarket steering wheel is one of those small things that can really help the driver interface with the car controls. It's not that the factory wheel is so bad, but aftermarket wheels usually allow you to grip the wheel better for more leverage. This is important when driving a car at the limit, as race tracks are usually bumpier than they appear. I like the wheels that have molded grips to hook your thumbs into, but some also have a molded grip for the entire hand.

Placing a strip of adhesive tape around the rim on the top center of the

A three-layer suit provides 20 to 30 seconds protection from fire, which is hopefully enough time to exit the car or receive help from the marshals.

wheel provides a straight-ahead reference point for the driver. Subconsciously, the driver knows the location of the tape mark, even when all crossed up, and uses it as a point of reference.

Different diameters are available to suit the driver's taste, and some models like the Momo Commando offer a squared-off lower portion that provides more clearance between the driver's thigh and the steering wheel. This can be important for preventing thigh-to-wheel contact while your feet are dancing across the pedals.

Most aftermarket steering wheels are not designed to accommodate the

An onboard fire suppression system can provide valuable seconds if a fire breaks out inside the car.

factory airbag. While this may not be important to you in the case of a track car, if your Mustang is your daily driver, you may not want to remove the airbag. While on the subject, I would remove the airbags on both sides of a Mustang that is primarily used as an open-track or drag car. Often in racing, a secondary collision occurs during an incident. If the airbag has been deployed in your face when you tapped the outside wall in corner four, it makes it darned difficult to try and bring the car under con-

trol when it comes ricocheting across the track towards the inside wall, still moving at 70 miles an hour! By the same token, airbags have saved countless lives on the street, so evaluate the best decision for your own scenario.

Driver's Suit

Eventually, if the Mustang owner becomes involved enough, he/she is going to require a driver's suit. I can't recall how many customers we've had that started with street cars, got involved in either open-track or drag racing, and within three or four years, they ended up with a full-blown racecar, complete with truck and trailer. If the day arrives when you need a driver's suit, a myriad of choices and price points are available. A triple-layer suit is the minimum specification suit that you should consider. Once again, a tag, this time from the SFI foundation, attests to a minimum standard for the suit. Just like with dress clothes, you can buy drivers suits off the rack, or custom tailored. In addition to the custom fit, tailored suits can also be ordered in a variety of custom designs and colors. With the advent of computerized material cutting, custom suit prices have come down very close to the cost of off-the-rack ones, making it easier than ever to justify a custom-fitted suit.

In the case of drag racing, the safety requirements dictate first a fire-resistant jacket, and then pants must be added as the speeds increase. Two-piece suits are more common in drag racing than single-piece suits, probably for this reason. Even if the series regulations do not specifically require it, at the point a drivers suit is mandatory, in my mind, so are fire resistant gloves and shoes. Protecting your torso and leaving your hands and feet exposed is pointless. In the event of a fire, your fire-resistant clothing is only going to buy you 20 or 30 seconds time to get out of the car and away from

the fire before you get burned. You need your hands and feet to get out of a car that is on fire. Enough said.

Fire System

The last safety item on our agenda is an on-board fire system. Although not specifically required by some series, an on-board fire system is essential in any track car. Aside from the obvious benefit to the driver in case of fire or accident, there are so many times when a car burns up due to electrical shorts or a fuel leak, and virtually no one insures their track car. An on-board system should include nozzles directed at the driver and in the engine compartment over the top of the engine. Aiming a nozzle towards the fuel tank is just wishful thinking. If the fuel tank gets involved, no way is the on-board fire system going to deal with that. As with the driver's suit, the on-board fire system is really designed to buy you 20 or 30 seconds until the track fire team can get to the scene. With this in mind, if you are about to have a big crash on the track, pull the fire system before you hit, if you can remember. Having an on-board fire system does no good at all if you are lying unconscious in the drivers seat, unable to trigger the system. Refilling the fire system is the least of your concerns if you have a major crash, so just pull it and hope you didn't really need to after all.

Sorry if it seems like I am being a harbinger of doom and gloom here, but you have to remember – all motorsport is potentially dangerous. If, like a Boy Scout, you are prepared, the likelihood of a positive outcome in a dangerous situation is much higher. Plus, I know as a driver, if my safety equipment is ship shape, if my seating position is comfortable, if I am properly restrained in the seat, I can drive faster and with more confidence – making it easier to kick your ass!

Get Involved!

The best part of Mustang ownership is the opportunity to get involved with other enthusiasts who share your interest. Whether it's car shows, cruises, or racing, something is available for everyone. Let's talk about some of the more popular activities.

MCA – Mustang Club of America

The Mustang Club of America has over 10,000 members worldwide, with local chapters in the USA, Canada, Mexico, and Colombia to name a few. In 2004, the MCA organized the 40th anniversary celebration for the Mustang in Nashville. In addition to celebrating the milestone events in Mustang history, the MCA holds regional and national events every year across America. MCA has a concours car show, with additional classes for modified cars, on-track events at locations such as Charlotte Motor Speedway, plus local activities unique to the chosen venue, that truly make these events a family affair. It's interesting to note the generations of Mustang owners at MCA events, often several in the same family. For young and old, boys and girls, the Mustang is a special car, one that transcends all the boundaries, equally adored by all.

Mustang Club of America
4051 Barrancas Ave. PMB 201
Pensacola, FL 32507
(850) 438-0626
www.mustang.org

Fun Ford Weekend

Bill Alexander of American Autosports has been organizing Fun Ford Weekends around the country for 15 years, adding one or two events a year. Needless to say, they have a full season. Every event includes heads-up Mustang drag racing, a car show, and swap meet. As a co-sponsor of the Modular Engine drag-racing class, along with Steeda, I am very proud to be associated with the Fun Ford Program. Ford has been directly involved in supporting the Fun Ford program, and helped raise the level of prize money available to the racer to the best anywhere. Payouts are up to $10,000 per class winner, and series champions walk away with the keys for a brand new Mustang. This is just one rea-

The Mustang Club of America organized the 40th anniversary of the Mustang get-together in Nashville. It was a great party, with lots of cars from all over North America attending.

Fun Ford embraced the 4.6L-powered Mustangs early on and formed the Mod Motor class to provide a venue for them. The class was sponsored from the beginning by Steeda/Sean Hyland, but the addition of some Ford backing enabled payouts of up to $10,000 per event.

Fun Ford Weekend Mustang Drag Racers compete in several heads up classes for cash prizes and bragging rights. (Photo courtesy Keplinger Designs)

The many heads-up classes for Mustangs are exciting for the fans to watch and fun for the drivers. The first man to the end wins – period.

son why the Fun Ford racing series attracts racers from outside the world of Mustangs to come and join our brand of racing. Many people wait all year, preparing their cars for the Fun Ford Weekend coming to their local track. The Spring Break Shootout, traditionally held in late February in Florida, is legendary, not only for the racing, but also for the after-racing party and freestyle burnout contest held at the local Hooters. Bill runs a first-class show – you should definitely come on out and see one.

FFW/American Autosports
    Productions
P.O. Box 911
Denham Springs, LA 70727-0997
(225) 664-0996
www.funfordevents.com
info@funfordevents.com

NMRA – National Mustang Racers Association

The NMRA holds heads-up drag racing, using classes similar to the Fun Ford format. These events take place at venues throughout the U.S., attracting some of the top Mustang drag racers. The NMRA has put together a solid championship in the past seven years. Racers and aftermarket manufacturers like to test their skills and abilities in a competitive arena, and the NMRA certainly provides that.

ProMedia Events Home Office
3518 West Lake Center Drive, Suite D
Santa Ana, CA 92704
(630) 595-2395
www.nmraracing.com
office@promediapub.com

WFC – World Ford Challenge

Eight years ago, George Gonzales had a concept of creating an amazing weekend of Mustang drag racing. First, he lined up the most prize money – winning the Pro 5.0 class at WFC pays $35,000 – big money by anyone's standards. The WFC event includes several classes of heads-up Mustang racing, a

The True Street class is where street-legal Mustangs must drive a 30-mile loop on public roads, and then run three passes without opening the hoods. Low nine-second ETs are required for an overall win in this class.

car show, and a manufacturers' midway. For the past several years, WFC has been held in St. Louis in mid May. George has certainly managed to create the largest single-weekend Mustang drag racing event anywhere.

World Race Events
11431 NW 34th Street
Miami, FL 33178
(305) 436-0996
(305) 436-5116 (Fax)

SCCA – Sports Car Club of America

The Sports Car Club of America (SCCA) organizes a variety of events, from entry-level autocross events, right up through Speed World Challenge professional road racing. Even if you don't want to compete, they have a spot for you. As a track marshal, you can get right up close to the action, and you get to hang around with all the racers, without having to actually race.

Autocross is a great entry-level motorsport, and a lot of people, myself included, got their start there. You can literally drive your street car in off the road and enter into timed competition on a pylon

This Steed-sponsored car is racing in the Speed World Challenge. It takes on full factory-sponsored cars and does quite well. It also serves as a test bed for their new suspension parts.

course laid out in a parking lot. It may look amateur, but don't kid yourself, top autocross drivers have amazing car control, able to place their car within fractions of an inch, every time they are on the course. SN95 Mustangs fit in several stock and modified classes, and are competitive cars at autocross events.

Club racing is sanctioned by SCCA at tracks across the country. It provides road racers an opportunity to race competitively without the expense of a traveling series. Those who wish to pursue higher goals can race within their division, and if successful enough, can earn a berth at the national runoffs held

every fall and compete to be a national champion. Mustangs have competed in the T1 Showroom Stock class, and are quite successful in A Sedan against Camaros and Firebirds.

Racers with enough budget can run in the Speed World Challenge, an SCCA Pro Racing category featuring a sprint race format, pitting themselves against some of the world's best road racers at venues right across the country. Given the budget required, and the list of manufacturers involved directly, Mustangs have not been contesting for podium positions in Speed World Challenge. But given the right resources, a good Mustang team

Larry Rehagen and Dean Martin have successfully campaigned Mustangs in the Grand Am Cup series for several years. These cars run three-hour endurance races across North America, racing at famed venues like Daytona, Watkins Glen, and Laguna Seca.

could compete equally with the Corvettes and Vipers in this series.

SCCA National Staff
Mailing Address:
P.O. Box 19400
Topeka, KS 66619-0400
Physical Address:
Building 300, B Street
Topeka, KS 66619
(785) 357-7222
(785) 232-7228 (Fax)
www.scca.org

Grand Am – Grand American Road Racing

Grand Am, the road-racing portion of the NASCAR empire, has an endurance road-racing series for street-based cars with allowable modifications. The races run in a three-hour format and attract some of the best professional road racers anywhere. Competing at famous venues like Daytona and Watkins Glen, many car manufacturers field factory-backed teams. Ford did not race directly in this series during the SN95 production, but private teams such as Multimatic and Rehagen Racing have won many races over the years with late-model Mustangs. The rules keep the playing field level, allowing driver talent and teamwork in the pits to determine the outcome of the races.

Grand American Road Racing
Association
1801 West International
Speedway Blvd.

Daytona Beach, FL 32114-1243
(386) 947-6681
(386) 947-6695 (Fax)
webmaster@grandamerican.com
www.grandamerican.com

NASA – National Auto Sport Association

The NASA American Iron series is a regional road-racing series with two classes: American Iron and American Iron Extreme. These classes pit Mustangs against Camaros in an epic battle. The cars are regulated for power output in American Iron class, keeping the costs in line and allowing driver talent, not checkbook size, to determine the winners. Mustangs have been a mainstay of

Ford didn't sponsor any Grand-Am Mustangs, but that didn't stop Rehagen and Martin numerous Grand Am podium finishes in their Cobra Cup car over the last few seasons.

this series since its inception, and it offers close racing at reasonable cost for many SN95 owners.

National Office
P.O. Box 21555
Richmond, CA 94820
(510) 232-6272
(510) 412-0549 (Fax)
www.nasaproracing.com
nasadaveho@yahoo.com

Racers chase each other around the houses in Gander Newfoundland during Targa Newfoundland. (Photo Credit - Jim Johnson for GOTNL [Targa on the Streets of Gander] Productions.)

Targa

There exists a type of competition similar to the real road racing that used to occur at the Mille Miglia and Targa Florio open-road races of the 1950s and 1960s. Targa competitions are essentially tarmac stage rallies run on public roads that are temporarily closed for competition. The Targa format requires the cars to leave at 30-second intervals, with the fastest cars seeded to the back. The roads are run with simple instructions from the organizers, and the shortest accumulated time on the stage determines the winner. The competition puts a premium on car-control skills, as the roads are run blind, and speeds can top 120 mph on narrow roads winding through villages. Mustangs have been quite suc-

A Cobra R plays in the puddles in New Zealand during the annual Targa New Zealand event. This particular Cobra R was one of the first Rs to be used in competition. In addition to Targa events, it presently competes in a New Zealand-based endurance race championship.

cessful in Targa competition. Races are held presently in New Zealand, Tasmania, and Newfoundland, Canada.

Targa Newfoundland
(709) 722 2413
(877) 332-2413
www.targanewfoundland.com
info@targanewfoundland.com
Dunlop Targa New Zealand
Club Targa Inc.
PO Box 72502
Papakura, Auckland 1730
New Zealand
+64 9 298 8266 (Fax)
www.targa.co.nz
Targa Tasmania
Octagon Hobart
136 Davey Street
Hobart, Tasmania, 7000
Australia

+61 3 6224 1512
+61 3 6224 3454 (Fax)
targa.info@octagon.com
www.targa.org.au

This Mustang is going 205 mph in the desert at the Silver State Classic race. Don't try this with your stock Mustang.

Silver State Challenge

The Silver State Challenge is an open-road event run on public roads, temporarily closed during the event, in Nevada. Competitors come from around the world to compete in this unique event, which has a history of cars in the unlimited class regularly exceeding 200 mph. Mustangs have had some success in this event, and the average speed classes range from 95 mph to unlimited, depending on experience and car preparation, so something suitable can be found for everyone here. I don't know if they still do it, but the local brothel in Ely used to have an award for the best looking car as voted by the ladies who worked there. The award given was for "services," redeemable at the establishment.

SCTA – Southern California Timing Association

The Southern California Timing Association organizes timed, top-speed meets at El Mirage dry lake in Southern California, and the famed Bonneville salt flats in Utah. The SCTA has a large assortment of classes for Mustangs, and is one of the last refuges for the amateur racer and hot rodder, a place where skill and ingenuity can still triumph over the almighty dollar.

SCTA – BNI
P.O. Box 10
Orosi, Ca. 93647
(559) 528-6279
(559) 528-9749 (Fax)
www.scta-bni.org
office@scta-bni.org

This is not an exhaustive look at all the opportunities for involvement, but rather a starting place, a sampler if you will, of the smorgasbord of events out there. Find what interests you, try it, and encourage others to do the same. Most of all – enjoy the ride.

Bonneville Salt Flats – the last bastion of the amateur racer. A Mustang can compete in many classes, depending on the modifications.

Project Car Build Ups

This section is an opportunity to look at some SN95 Mustangs modified to suit their owner's requirements. These cars represent some well-sorted packages that can provide valuable insight into which parts combinations are effective for different activities.

Open-Track '99 Cobra

This car started as a street car, complete with child seat and all. Now it's four years later, there isn't even a back seat, and the car hasn't seen the street in two years. Now that the evolution is mostly complete, this car is fast. 1:36 at Mosport is pretty stout, made possible by its 400 hp and light weight. The chassis is well sorted on this car, and it's an easy car to drive quickly. This father and son duo spend a good deal of quality time together at tracks all over the eastern U.S. and Canada. In this respect alone it has to be considered an unqualified success.

Specifications
Chassis: Kenny Brown subframe connectors, jacking rails, and extreme matrix system, custom roll cage
Body:
Carbon fiber doors
Carbon fiber hood
Carbon fiber trunk lid
Carbon fiber roof panel
Lexan quarter and rear windows

Suspension:
Griggs tubular K-member and tubular front lower control arms
Kenny Brown tubular rear upper and lower control arms
Koni double adjustable coil-over front struts
Koni double adjustable rear dampers with coil overs
1.375" front anti-roll bar, stock rear anti-roll bar
Aluminum subframe bushings
Spherical joints in rear uprights

Brakes:
Brembo Cobra R front brakes with 13" rotors
Stock rear brakes
Hawk brake pads front and rear braided stainless flex lines
Cobra R carbon fiber brake ducts
Motul brake fluid
Wheels/Tires:
Ford Racing 17 x 9-inch Cobra R wheels
275/40/17 Hoosier tires
Engine:
Sean Hyland 5.0L (3.70" bore, 3.54" stroke)

The extensive roll cage on this car contributes to the overall stiffness of the chassis, which is part of the reason it handles so well.

Forged steel crankshaft
Forged steel connecting rods
Forged pistons
Ported cylinder heads and intake manifold

SHM camshafts
Long-tube 1-3/4" to 1-7/8" step-tube race headers
3-inch collectors and boom tubes

Fuel System:
Bosch fuel pump
Braided stainless fuel lines
Billet fuel rails
Billet fuel regulator
42-lb/hr injectors
Custom chip
Transmission:
Tremec T-56 6-speed
Terminator aluminum flywheel
11" heavy-duty clutch assembly
Differential:
3.73:1 gear ratio
Torsen 31-spline differential and axles
SHM differential cooler

A father and son team drives this car all over North America to open track events. It sure beats the heck out of golf!

The front end of this track Mustang uses a Kenny Brown K-member, Koni double-adjustable dampers with coil-over conversion, and a nifty fabricated adjustable anti-roll bar.

The abbreviated dash saves some weight, and the removable steering wheel makes ingress and egress, not to mention maintenance, much easier.

Under the hood is your basic Sean Hyland-built 4.6L Cobra engine, bored out to 5.0L. With great heads and cams it makes a reliable 400 hp.

Street Racer '96 Cobra

This '96 Cobra has evolved over several years to become a very quick street-driven Mustang, capable of 9.50 ETs at over 150 mph. This car still has the full factory interior, plus a roll cage, and yet is purposely understated, with no monster tach on the dash or unnecessary items to draw attention to the car. Only the factory Mystic paint and the wheels and tires give some hint of the cars potential. Under the hood however, it's a different story, with a full-on 4-valve engine, supercharged with an F-2 Procharger, cog-drive belts, sheetmetal intake, and a C4 transmission with transbrake. This is one cool Mustang. It can cruise the strip, and lay down the number when required, but like most nocturnal animals, is rarely seen during the daylight hours.

This '96 Mystic Cobra looks pretty stock on the outside, but with 900 hp on tap, 9.50-seond ETs at 150 mph are not out of the ordinary.

Specifications
Chassis:
Subframe connectors
8-point roll cage
Suspension:
Tubular front crossmember
Coilover front suspension
QA1 adjustable struts
Steeda adjustable upper rear control arms
Lakewood lower rear control arms
QA1 adjustable rear dampers
TRZ adjustable rear anti-roll bar
Brakes:
Front and rear Aerospace billet drag brakes
Manual master cylinder kit
Braided stainless flex lines
Motul brake fluid
Wheels/Tires:
Bogart 15 x 3.5-inch front and
15 x 10-inch rear lightweight wheels
Mickey Thompson 26 x 7.50 front tires and 28 x 10.5-inch rear slicks
Engine:
Sean Hyland 4.6L Cobra engine
.020-inch oversize forged pistons
Billet connecting rods

From the rear, the only clues as to this thing's potential are the master electrical switch and the fuel pump.

A roll cage now surrounds the stock rear seat.

The interior is fairly stock, save for a 6-point roll cage and some competition seat belts. There's no aftermarket tachometer and the car still has all the stock carpet and seats – it's a sleeper.

The only external clues to the car's potential are the Bogart wheels and Mickey Thompson front runners and 28 x 10.5W slicks in the rear.

The 4-inch intercooler ducting supplies cool air to the throttle body. Notice the straps restraining the ducts from slipping apart during air pressure spikes. Boost pressure is set at 30 psi.

Under the hood we find a Sean Hyland-built Cobra engine with sheet metal intake and a cog-driven Procharger F2 supercharger.

Forged steel crankshaft
Ported cylinder heads with oversize
Stainless valves
Dual valve springs with titanium retainers
SHM camshafts
Hogan sheet metal intake manifold
Accufab throttle body
ATI F2M supercharger

Accufab 50-mm cog drive
SHM intercooler
Electric water pump
Fuel System:
Weldon fuel pump
Sump fuel tank
Billet fuel rails
83-lb/hr Siemens injectors
FAST fuel injection

Braided stainless fuel lines
Transmission:
C4 with transbrake
5,500-rpm stall converter
B&M shifter
Rear Axle:
Ford 8.8 inch
4.10:1 gear ratio
31-spline spool and axles

Street/Show '03 Cobra

This particular '03 Cobra is a show car, used to showcase the owner's electronic products at trade shows. It's also driven at open-track events, the occasional Friday night at the drags, and of course, on the street. This car has been modified to handle and brake well at the track, it has some neat custom touches like the Lambo-style doors and the Stalker body kit, but it also boasts a built engine with a Kenne-Bell Blowzilla supercharger plus nitrous. It makes over 750 hp at the flywheel when placed on kill mode. A dual-program chip allows detuning the engine to just over 600 hp for use on the street and at open-track events. This Mustang is proof positive you can have your cake and eat it too!

Specifications
Chassis:
Subframe connectors
Rear shock tower brace
Modified strut tower brace
Body:
Cervini Stalker body kit
Shaved door handles
Lambo-style door hinges
Interior:
Sparco Milano seats
Momo Commando steering wheel
Suspension:
SHM springs
Koni dampers
Caster/camber plates
SHM IRS subframe bushings
KB Forward torque brace
Solid pinion bushings
SHM delrin rear control arms bushings
Brakes:
Baer 13-inch front kit
Baer rear rotors
Hawk brake pads
Stainless flex lines
Motul brake fluid
Wheels/Tires:
SSR 18 x 9-inch front and
18 x 10.5-inch rear 3-piece wheels
Pirelli P Zero Corsa 265/35/18 front

This '03 Cobra is multi-use – show car, daily driver, and open-track racer. The body kit is a tasteful addition that adds to the overall look of the car.

The Lambo-style door conversion with shaved door handles creates a nice custom touch to this car.

and 295/30/18 rear tires
Engine:
Sean Hyland-built '03 Cobra engine
.020-inch oversize forged pistons
Forged connecting rods
Stainless valves
Kenne Bell 2.4L supercharger (20 psi)
Dual pass heat exchanger
3-core aluminum radiator
Fuel System:
Sump tank

Billet fuel rails
60-lb/hr Siemens injectors
-8 stainless fuel line
Weldon fuel pump
Transmission:
Original T56 6-speed
Steeda shifter
Rear Axle:
3.73:1 gear ratio
Eaton 31-spline differential

A Baer brake upgrade is helpful when open tracking the car, as are the 18-inch Pirelli P Zero Corsa tires mounted on three-piece SSR rims.

The interior includes leather Sparco seats with four-point seat belts and a Momo Commando steering wheel.

Under the hood, we have a Sean Hyland-built engine, Kenne Bell twin-screw supercharger upgrade, and an upgraded fuel system to support all the additional power.

A 75-hp dry nitrous system is plumbed in front of the Accufab throttle body, adding a top end burst of speed when required.

The Classis Design Concepts light bar looks racy, but is for show only – it does not provide any rollover protection.

This ' 00 Mustang GT was a project car for the television show Sports Car Revolution. We showcased the Mustang GT as a multi-use sports car, capable of being a daily driver, weekend drag racer, and open track toy. Good ETs require some starting-line traction, in this case supplied by Mickey Thompson drag radial tires. Heating the tires with a burnout is key to a good 60-ft time.

'00 GT Daily Driver

This '00 GT was purchased off a used car lot and transformed into a daily driver and weekend drag and open-track racer. Through selecting complementary components, the car has become a very versatile piece. The budget for the entire project is well within many enthusiasts' grasp, especially if you can only afford one car and want to do many different things with it. This Mustang is just a great everyday car.

Specifications:
Chassis:
Subframe connectors
Strut brace
Suspension:
Steeda springs
Front anti-roll bar
Adjustable rear anti-roll bar
Caster/camber plates
Lower A-arm bushings
Offset rack bushings
Adjustable upper rear control arms
Billet lower rear control arms
X2 ball joints, bumpsteer kit

Koni dampers
Brakes
StopTech 13-inch front rotors and 4-piston calipers
Satisfied Gran Sport front and rear brake pads
Braided stainless brake lines
Motul brake fluid
Wheels/Tires:
ROH 17 x 9-inch wheels
Toyo RA1 275/40/17 tires
Engine:
Sean Hyland 4.6L
Forged rods and pistons
Forged steel crankshaft
Stainless valves
Ported heads
COMP Cams camshafts
Accufab throttle body
JBA headers
H pipe
Cat-back exhaust
Fuel System:
Ford Racing 24-lb/hr injectors
2003 Cobra fuel pump
Transmission:
Steeda shifter, cable, quadrant, and firewall adjuster

The brakes were upgraded with a Brembo Cobra R 13-inch brake kit. This required a wheel with spokes designed to clear the big brakes, in this case ROH 17- x 9-inch wheels shod with 275/40/17 Toyo RA1 tires, perfect for open-track use.

2003 Cobra aluminum flywheel and clutch assembly
Rear Axle:
4.10:1 gear ratio
Auburn ECTED electronic limited-slip differential
31-spline alloy axles
Aluminum driveshaft
Safety loop

The body was about the only part of the car not modified, relying on the addition of some good-looking wheels and tires, combined with the lowered stance to create a classic look.

Once finished, we had a 12-second street car – not too shabby for a street-driven GT still capable of pulling down 25 mpg.

Steeda 17- x 9-inch Ultralite wheels with 274/40/17 Toyo RA1 tires provide the level of grip required, while the StopTech 13.5-inch brakes provide the "whoa" required at the Targa rally.

'01 Mustang Targa Car

This car started as a base GT purchased off a used car lot. Its drivetrain was transplanted from a previous Targa car and the chassis was updated at the same time. Targa competition is like a Pro Rally, sort of. The roads are all paved and closed to the public during the event. Presently, Targa events take place in Canada, Tasmania, and New Zealand. Unlike a Pro Rally, the fastest competitors start last, which means that by the time they start, the corners are covered in loose gravel, requiring a careful approach. So, with this in mind, this Mustang is set up similar to a road-racecar, but with more ground clearance. It is softly sprung to help get the power down on bumpy surfaces. The supercharged Cobra engine produces

This '01 GT has been prepared as a Targa car, specifically to compete in the Targa Newfoundland tarmac rally. The body modifications include a Cobra R type splitter, '03 Cobra fascia and hood, and a Cobra R rear wing, all designed to help aero at 130 mph.

Under the hood we find a Sean Hyland-built Cobra engine with a Paxton supercharger. The 655-hp engine supplies more than ample power for open-road races.

The inside of the car boasts a substantial roll cage, OMP race seats, five-point competition belts, and an onboard fire system.

The Fluidyne three-core aluminum radiator and AFCO supercharger heat exchanger increase the thermal capacity of the cooling system, which is essential when the power output is increased.

Holding the car up off the ground, we find Koni dampers, Eibach racing springs, and a complement of Steeda suspension components.

Inside the car, it's all business. In addition to the stock instrumentation, we find AutoMeter gauges in the center console, plus a rally computer on the passenger, sorry, I mean co-driver's side.

625 hp, which is plenty to squirt between the corners. Rugged one-piece wheels are used to withstand encounters with curbs, and the exhaust has been shielded to prevent damage from jumps. The Mustang has been outfitted with a full roll cage, seats, safety equipment, plus two-way radios and a rally computer. The objective here is to have a tough and durable car that can take a pounding day after day for a week.

Specifications:
Chassis:
Subframe connectors
Full roll cage
Body:
Cobra R rear wing
Optional Cobra R front splitter
Removable lexan side windows

Interior:
OMP race seats
5-point belts
Sparco steering wheel
Rally computer
On-board fire system
Suspension:
Steeda adjustable upper rear control arms
Billet lower control arms
Eibach springs
Koni dampers
Stock front and rear anti-roll bars
Urethane suspension bushings
Bumpsteer kit
X2 ball joints
Caster/camber plates
Brakes:
StopTech 13.5-inch rotors and 4-piston front calipers
Hawk pads front and rear
Stainless brake lines
Motul fluid

Wheels/Tires:
Steeda Ultralite 17 x 9-inch wheels
Toyo 275/40/17 RA1 tires
Engine:
Sean Hyland 4.6L Cobra engine
.020 oversize forged pistons
Forged rods
Forged steel crank
Blower cams
Paxton Novi supercharger (18 psi)
Sean Hyland air-to-air intercooler
Transmission:
T45 5-speed
'03 Cobra flywheel/clutch package
Billet clutch quadrant
Firewall adjuster
Rear Axle:
3.73:1 gear ratio
Tractech C locker differentia
31-spline alloy axles

Accufab LLC
1514-B E. Francis St.
Ontario, CA 91761
(909) 930-1751
www.accufabracing.com

ADDCO Manufacturing, Inc.
1596 Linville Falls Hwy.
Linville, NC 28646
(800) 621-8916
(828) 733-1562 (Fax)
www.addco.net

Aeromotive
218 W 74th St.
Kansas City, MO 64114
(816) 333-7300
www.aeromotive.com

**Alatec Racing
(now Pentacon)**
1926 Peach St.
Erie, PA 16502
(814) 456-3855
www.pentacon.com

Automotive Racing Products
1863 Eastman Ave
Ventura, CA 93003
(805) 339-2200
www.arpbolts.com

Accessible Technologies (ProCharger)
14801 W. 114th Terrace
Lenexa, KS 66215
(913) 338 2886
www.procharger.com

Auburn Gear Inc.
400 East Auburn Drive
Auburn, IN 46706 - 3499
(260) 925-3200
(260) 925-4725 (Fax)
www.auburngear.com
agdiffs@auburngear.com

Autotronic Controls Corp.
1490 Henry Brennan Dr.
El Paso, TX 79936
(915) 857 5200
www.msdignition.com

Autopower Industries, Inc.
3424 Picket St.
San Diego, CA 92110
(619) 297-3300
(619) 297-9765 (Fax)
www.autopowerindustries.com

Canton Racing Products
232 Branford Rd.
North Brandford, CT 06471
(203) 481 9460
www.cantonracing
products.com

Car Sound
22961 Arroyo Vista
Rancho Santa Margaritta, CA 92688
(949) 858-5900
www.magnaflow.com

**Castrol
BP Lubricants USA, Inc.**
1500 Valley Road
Wayne, NJ 07470
(800) 462-0835
www.castrolusa.com

Competition Cams
3406 Democrat Rd.
Memphis TN 38118
(901) 795-2400
www.compcams.com

CARRILLO Industries
990 Calle Amanecer
San Clemente, CA 92673
(949) 498-1800
(949) 498-2355 (Fax)
sales@carrilloind.com
www.carrilloind.com

Crane Cams
P.O. Box 860426
Orlando, FL 32886-042
(904) 252-1151
www.cranecams.com

Detroit Locker
31900 Sherman Avenue
Madison Heights, MI 48071
(248) 776-5700
(248) 776-5702 (Fax)
cs@detroitlocker.com
www.detroitlocker.com

DiabloSport
1865 S.W 4th Avenue,
Suite #D2
Delray Beach, FL 33444
(561) 908-0040
(561) 908-0051 (Fax)
www.diablosport.com

FIA – Federation Internationale De L'Automobile
8, Place de la Concorde
75008 Paris
France
+33 1 43 12 44 55
+33 1 43 12 44 66 (Fax)
www.fia.com

Fikse USA, Inc.
6851 S 220th Street
Kent, WA 98032
(253) 872-3888
(253) 437-0187 (Fax)
www.fikse.com

Fluidyne High Performance
2605 E Cedar St.
Ontario, CA 91761
(909) 923-9595
www.fluidyne.com

Flowmaster Mufflers Inc.
100 Stony Point Road, Ste 125
Santa Rosa, CA 95401
(800) 544-4761
(707) 544-4784 (Fax)
www.flowmastermufflers.com

Ford Racing Performance Parts (FRPP)
38000 Amrhein
Livonia, MI 48150-1016
(734)-458-0600
(734)-458-0550 (Fax)
frtmail@ford.com
www.fordracingparts.com

Goodridge
20309 Gramercy Place
Torrance, CA 90501
(310) 533-1924
www.goodridge.net

GranSport Performance Brakes
805 Education Rd.
Cornwall, Ontario
Canada
K6H 6C7
(613) 933.3300
(613) 933.3365 (Fax)
custserv@gransportbrakes.com
www.gransportbrakes.com

Kenny Brown Performance
57 Gasoline Alley
Indianapolis, IN 46222
(317) 247-5320
(317) 247-5347 (Fax)
www.kennybrown.com

Kirkey Racing Fabrication Inc.
P.O. Box 445
Rooseveltown, NY 13683
(800) 363-4885
(800) 829-7072 (Fax)
www.kirkeyracing.com
kirkey@kirkeyracing.com

Kooks Custom Headers
59 Cleveland Ave.
Bay Shore, NY 11706
(631) 586-9002
www.kookscustomheaders.com

KONI North America
1961 International Way
Hebron, KY 41048
(859) 586-4100
(859) 334-3340 (Fax)
www.koni-na.com

Kromer Kraft
1750 Harding Ave.
Girard, OH 44420
(330) 539-5053
www.kromerkraft.com

KYB America LLC
140 N. Mitchell Court
Addison, IL 60101
(630) 620-5555
www.kyb.com

Moroso
80 Carter Drive
Guilford, CT 06437-211
(203) 453-6571
www.moroso.com

Moton Suspension Technology Inc.
5174 Performance Drive, Suite A
Cumming, GA 30040
(770) 886-8777
(770) 886-8776 (Fax)
motonusa@bellsouth.net
www.motonsuspension.com

Mosport International Raceway
Bowmanville, Ontario
Canada
(905) 983-9141
www.mosport.com
info@mosport.com

Multimatic Inc.
85 Valleywood Drive
Markham, Ontario
Canada
L3R 5L9
(905) 470-2909
(905) 470-0169 (Fax)
info@multimatic.com
www.multimatic.com

NGK Spark Plugs (U.S.A.), Inc.
6 Whatney
Irvine, CA 92618
(949) 855-8278
(949) 855-8395
www.ngksparkplugs.com

NHRA - National Hot Rod Association
2035 Financial Way
Glendora, CA 91741
(626) 914-4761
(626) 963-5360 (Fax)
www.nhra.com
nhra@nhra.com

Nitto Tire N. America Inc.
6261 Katella Ave. Suite 2C
Cypress, CA 90630
(510) 445-5468
(510) 445-5480 (Fax)
www.nittotire.com

OMP America LLC
7056 Portal Way
Building I, Unit 1
Ferndale, WA 98248
(360) 366-0959
(360) 336-0590 (Fax)
www.ompamerica.com
sales@ompamerica.com

Paxton Automotive Corp.
P.O. Box 57
Camarillo, CA 93011-005
(805) 987-8660
www.paxtonauto.com

Precision Turbo
616A S Main St.
P.O. Box 425
Hebron, IN 46341
(219) 996-7832
www.precisionte.com

Snell Memorial Foundation
3628 Madison Ave., Suite 11
North Highlands, CA 95660
(916) 331-5073
(916) 331-0359 (Fax)
www.smf.org
info@smf.org

Sparco Motor Sports Inc.
1852 Kaiser Ave.
Irvine, CA 92614
1-800-224-RACE
(949) 797-1755 (Fax)
www.sparcousa.com
info@sparcousa.com

Spearco / Turbonetics
2255 Agate Ct.
Simi Valley, CA 93065
(805) 581-0333
www.turbonetics.com

Stage 8
15 Chestnut Ave.
San Rafael, CA 94901
(415) 485-5340
www.stage8.com

Steeda
1351 N.W. Steeda Way
Pompano Beach, FL 33069
(954) 960-0774
www.steeda.com

StopTech
3541 Unit A, Lomita Blvd.,
Torrance, CA 90505
(310) 325-4799
(310) 325-6627 (Fax)
www.stoptech.com
sales@stoptech.com

SVTOA – Special Vehicle Team Owners Association
PO Box 910505
San Diego, CA 92191
(866) 377-8862
(858) 777-6563 (Fax)
www.svtoa.com
info@svtoa.com

Tokico USA Inc.
1330 Storm Parkway
Torrence, CA 90501
(310) 534-4934
(310) 898-3084
www.tokicogasshocks.com

BBS of America, Inc.
5320 BBS Drive
Braselton, GA 30517
(877) 832-8209
(770) 967-9866
sales@bbs-usa.com
www.bbs-usa.com

B&M Racing & Performance Products LLC
9142 Independence Ave.
Chatsworth, CA 91311
(818) 882-6422
(818) 882-3616 (Fax)
www.bmracing.com

Bell Racing, Inc.
116 East Neal Drive
Rantoul, IL 61866
(800) 237-2700
www.bellracing.com

BF Goodrich
P.O. Box 19001
Greenville, SC 29602-9001
(877) 788-8899
www.bfgoodrichtires.com

Bilstein
14102 Stowe Drive
Poway, CA 92064
(858) 386-5900
www.bilstein.com

Borla
5901 Edison Dr.
Oxnard, CA 93033
(805) 986-8600
www.borla.com

Brembo Headquarters
Via Brembo N. 25
24035 Curno
Bergamo
Italy
Tel. 0039 035 605 111
U.S. Phone: (800)-325-3994
www.brembo.com

Bridgestone
P.O. Box 7988
Chicago, IL 60680-9534
(800) 367-3872
(800) 760-7859 (Fax)
www.bridgestone-firestone.com

Driveshaft Shop, The
210A Blydenburgh rd.
Islandia, NY 11749
(631) 348-1818
(631) 348-1844 (Fax)
driveshaftshop@hotmail.com
www.driveshaftshop.com

Earl's Performance
189 West Victoria St.
Long Beach, CA 90805
(800) 421-2712
www.earlsperformance.com

Eaton Corporation
1101 W. Hanover
Marshall, MI 49068
(269) 789-3207
(269) 789-3201 (Fax)
www.eaton.com

Edelbrock
2700 California St.
Torrance, CA 90503
(310) 781-2222
www.edelbrock.com

Eibach Springs
17817 Gillette Ave.
Irvine, CA 92714
(951) 256-8300
(951) 256-8319 (Fax)
www.eibach.com

Electromotive Inc.
9131 Centerville Rd.
Manassas, VA 20110
(703) 331-0100
www.electromotive-inc.com

Energy Suspension
1131 Via Callejon
San Clemente, CA 92673 US
(949) 393-5361
hyperflex@energysuspension.com
www.energysuspension.com

Exedy - Daikin Clutch Corporation
8601 Haggerty Rd
Belleville, MI 48111
(800) 346-6091
(734) 397-7300 (Fax)
AftermarketSales@dcc-us.com
www.daikin-clutch.com

H&R Special Springs, LP
3815 Bakerview Spur #7
Bellingham, WA 98226
(888) 827-8881
(360) 738-8889 (Fax)
www.hrsprings.com

Holley Performance
NW 7942
P.O. Box 1450
Minneapolis, MN 55485-794
(800) 638-0032
www.holley.com

Hotchkis Performance
12035 Burke Street Suite 13
Santa Fe Springs, CA 90670
(877) 466-7655
doliver@hotchkis.net
www.hotchkis.net

HRE Performance Wheels
2453 Cades Way, Bldg. A,
Vista, CA 92081
(760) 598.1960
(760) 598-5885 (Fax)
sales@hrewheels.com
www.hrewheels.com

Innovative Turbo Systems
845 Easy St.
Simi Valley, CA 93065
(805) 526-5400
www.innovativeturbo.com

J.E Pistons
15312 Connector Lane
Huntington Beach, CA 92649
(714) 898-9763
www.jepistons.com

Jaz Products Inc
P.O. Box 3504
Thousand Oaks, CA 91359
(805) 525-8800
1-800-525-8133
www.jazproducts.com

JBA Automotive Engineered
7149 Mission Gorge, Suite D
San Diego, CA 92120-110
(619) 229-7797
www.jbaheaders.com

Kenne Bell
10743 Bell Court
Rancho Cucamonga, CA 91730
(909) 941-6646
www.kennebell.net

Motul
119 Boulevard Felix Faure
Aubervilliers, 93303
France
+33.148117000
+33.148332879 (Fax)
www.motul.com

Mr. Gasket
8700 Brook Park Rd.
Cleveland, OH 44129
(216) 688-8300
www.mrgasket.com

Manley Performance
P.O. Box 799
1960 Swarthmore Ave.
Lakewood, NJ 08701
(800) 526-1362
www.manleyperformance.com

Maximum Motorsports, Inc.
3430 Sacramento Dr., Unit D
San Luis Obispo, CA 93401
(805) 544-8748
(805) 544-8645 (Fax)
sales@maximummotorsports.com
www.maximummotorsports.com

Mickey Thompson Performance Tires and Wheels
4670 Allen Road
Stow, OH 44224
(330) 928-9092
(330) 928-0503 (Fax)
www.mickeythompsontires.com

MOMO U.S.A. Inc.
25471 Arctic Ocean Dr.
Lake Forest, CA 92630
(949) 380-7556
(949) 380-7256 (Fax)
www.momo.it

Morana Racing Engines
6453 Kingston Rd.
Scarborough, Ontario
Canada
M1C 1L2
(416) 412-2815
(416) 412-2927 (Fax)
www.moranav6racing.com

Moroso
80 Carter Drive
Guilford, CT 06437-2116
(203) 453-6571
(203) 453-6906 (Fax)
www.moroso.com

Prothane
3560 Cadillac Ave.
Costa Mesa, CA 92626
1-888-PROTHANE
(714) 979-3468 (Fax)
www.prothane.com

RECARO North America Inc.
3275 Lapeer Road West,
Auburn Hills, MI 48326
(248) 364-3818
(248) 364-3804 (Fax)
www.recaro-nao.com

Russell
2301 Dominguez Way
Torrance, CA 90501
310-781-2222
310-320-1187 (Fax)

Sabelt S.p.A.
Via G. Rossa 10,
10024 Moncalieri (TO - Italy)
+39 011 6477911
+39 011 6477999 (fax)
www.sabelt.com

Saleen, Inc. Headquarters
76 Fairbanks
Irvine, CA 92618-1602
(949) 597-4900
(949) 597-0301 (Fax)
info@saleen.com
www.saleen.com

SCT - Superchips Custom Tuning
134 Baywood Avenue
Longwood, FL 32750
(407) 774-2447
(407) 260-6275 (Fax)
sales@sctflash.com
www.sctflash.com

Sean Hyland Motorsport
691 Jack Ross Ave.
Woodstock, Ontario
Canada
N5Y 2Z2
(519) 421-2291
www.seanhylandmotorsport.com

Simpson
328 FM 306
New Braunfels, TX 78130
(830) 625.1774
(830) 625.3269 (Fax)
www.simpsonraceproducts.com
texassales@teamsimpson.com

Torsen Traction
2 Jet View Drive
Rochester, NY 14624-4904
(585) 464-5000
(585) 328-5477 (Fax)
torsen@torsen.com
www.torsen.com

Tremec TTC
23382 Commerce Drive
Farmington Hills, MI 48335
(865) 329-5090
(248) 471-3722 (Fax)
www.ttcautomotive.com

TRZ Motorsports
Kissimmee, FL 34744
(407) 933-7385
(407) 933-7589 (Fax)
trzmotorsports@yahoo.com
www.trzmotorsports.com

Vortech Engineering Inc.
1650 Pacific Ave.
Channel Islands, CA 93033-990
(805) 247-0226
www.vortecheng.com

Watkins Glen International
2790 County Route 16
Watkins Glen, NY 14891
(607) 535-2486
(607) 535-8918 (Fax)
racing@theglen.com
www.theglen.com

Weldon Pump
P.O. Box 46579
640 Golden Oak
Oakwood Village OH 44146
(440) 232-2282
www.weldonpumps.com

Wellman Products Group / Hawk Performance
6180 Cochran Rd.
Solon, OH 44139
(440) 528-4000
(440) 528-4099 Fax
www.hawkperformance.com

Wilwood Engineering
4700 Calle Bolero
Camarillo, CA 93012
(805) 388-1188
(805) 388-4938 (Fax)
customerreply@wilwood.com
www.wilwood.com

Aerodynamic Downforce:
When air flows over an object the pressure difference between the top and bottom surface (area) of the object will generate a resultant force. The resultant force may be acting upwards, commonly referred to as lift, or acting downwards, commonly referred to as downforce.

Aspect Ratio:
The relationship between the section height and section width of a tire expressed as a percentage of section width. E.g. a 275/40R17 tire specifies that the section height is 40 percent of the section width (275 mm). This gives a section height of 110 mm.

Atmospheric Pressure:
The pressure exerted on the Earth's surface caused by the weight of the air in the atmosphere. At sea level, this pressure is 14.7 psi. Atmospheric pressure decreases as the elevation increases.

Bead Seat:
The inner ledge portion of the wheel rim where the tire bead rests adjacent to the wheel flange.

Bumpsteer:
The tendency of a vehicle to suddenly change direction when hitting a bump or dip in the road, without the driver implementing a steering input. This condition is caused by uneven changes in toe as the suspension moves through its range of motion. Ideally bumpsteer is set to zero for performance applications.

Camber:
The angle of the wheel relative to vertical, when viewed from the front or rear of the vehicle. Negative camber is when the top of the wheel is angled towards the chassis. Positive camber is when the top of the wheel is angled away from the chassis.

Castor:
The angle to which the steering pivot axis is tilted forward or rearward from vertical, when viewed from the side of the vehicle. If the pivot axis is angled towards the rear of the vehicle, then the caster is positive. If the pivot axis is angled towards the front of the vehicle, then the caster is negative.

Coil Spring:
A type of spring made of wound heavy-gauge steel wire used to support the weight of the vehicle. The spring may be located between the control arm and chassis, the axle and chassis, or around a MacPherson strut. Coil springs may be conical or spiral wound, constant or variable rate, and wound with variable pitch spacing or variable thickness wire.

Contact Patch:
The contact area or tire print made by the tire on the ground. The contact patch changes shape as the cornering, braking and acceleration driving forces exerted on the tire change.

Damper (Shock Absorber):
Used primarily to dampen suspension oscillations. Shock absorbers respond only to motion. Some dampers may be gas charged to increase their performance. The damping effect is noticeable only during suspension movment.

Drag:
Drag is an aerodynamic force that opposes an objects motion through the air. The aerodynamic drag generated by an object is opposite to the direction of travel, thereby impeding its motion.

End Plate:
Typically a flat vertical rectangular plate attached to the ends of a wing. Designed to improve the effectiveness of the wing profile (increase the lift/drag ratio).

Front Splitter:
A flat surface parallel to the ground and underbody of the vehicle. A front splitter will typically extend slightly forward of the front bumper cover outline and somewhat rearward towards the front axle centerline, when viewed from the top of the vehicle. The device is intended to restrict the air from flowing underneath the vehicle thereby reducing or eliminating high-speed front-end lift. A well-designed splitter will generate downforce.

Gear Ratio:
The ratio between the number of teeth on a gear set. A rear end may have a 3.73:1 gear ratio. "Lower" gears have higher numbers.

Half Shaft:
The name given to either of the two driveshafts running from the differential to the rear wheels in an IRS vehicle.

IRS:
Independent Rear Suspension. When the rear wheels can act independently of one another. The only linkage joining the rear wheel pair would be the rear sway-bar.

Knocking (Detonation):
A noise caused by gasoline in the cylinders burning too quickly. Also known as detonation.

MacPherson Strut:
Instead of an upper control arm there is a strut, a slider or an infinitely long upper control arm, acting as the upper mounting point. The damper internals are contained within the strut housing. The major comprise of the strut-type suspension is that the tire loses camber rather then gaining camber as the wheel travels upwards (bump).

OBD II:
Onboard Diagnostics II. A second-generation engine diagnostic system required on all 1996 and newer vehicles.

Octane Number:
The rating number that indicates a gasoline's ability to resist knocking. The higher the rating, the greater the ability to resist to knocking.

Oversteer:
An oversteering car is sometimes said to be "loose", because its tail tends to swing wide. This handling condition is caused by the slip angle of the rear tires being greater than the slip angle of the front tires.

Rear Wing:
Most commonly mounted near the roofline on the rear of a vehicle. Intended to generate high-speed downforce at the cost of slightly increased drag.

Rebound:
A term commonly used to describe the movement of the suspension, as the wheel travels downwards away from the fender well.

Ride Height:
The distance between a specific location on the chassis, suspension, or body and the ground. An often-used term for chassis setup.

Roll Cage:
A network of tubing arranged inside the body of the vehicle. Designed to protect the driver during an accident and to increase the stiffness of the chassis.

Scrub Radius:
The distance between the extended centerline of the steering pivot axis and the centerline of the tire's contact patch, when viewed from the top of the vehicle on the ground plane. If the steering centerline is inboard of the tire centerline, the scrub radius is positive. If the steering centerline is outboard of the tire centerline, the scrub radius is negative. Rear-wheel drive cars generally have a positive scrub radius while FWD cars usually have zero or a negative scrub radius. Using wheels of different offset than stock can alter the vehicles scrub radius.

SLA:
A front suspension design using a long lower control arm and short upper control arm, allowing the tire the gain camber as the wheels travels upwards (bump). Typically referred to as Short long arm suspension (SLA).

Solid Axle:
When the rear wheel pair is rigidly connected to one another via axle housing. Most Mustang, those without IRS, have solid axles.

Anti-Roll Bar:
A tubular or solid round bar connected to a wheel pair, used in a suspension system to control body roll. An anti-roll bar may be used on the front and/or rear suspension to help keep the body flat as the vehicle rounds a corner. Its stiffness maybe changed in order to adjust the balance of the vehicle while cornering.

Sprung Mass:
Typically considered as the mass of the vehicle supported on the springs.

Thrust Angle:
The angle between the thrust line and centerline of the vehicle. If the thrust line is to the right of the centerline, the angle is said to be positive. If the thrust line is to the left of center, the angle is negative. It is caused by rear wheel or axle misalignment and causes the steering to pull or lead to one side or the other.

Toe:
When a pair of wheels are adjusted so that the front of the tires are pointing slightly towards each other, when viewed from the top of the vehicle, the wheel pair is said to have toe-in. If the front of the tires are pointing away from each other, when viewed from the top of the vehicle, the wheel pair is said to have toe-out.

Torque Wrench:
A special wrench with a built-in indicator that shows you how much force you're applying to a bolt. Most commonly described in ft-lb, in-lb or N-m of torque. A torque wrench should be used for all critical bolt applications e.g., brake system, suspension components, and when tightening lug nuts.

Understeer:
An understeering car is sometimes said to "push", because it resists turning and tends to go straight. This handling condition is caused by the slip angle of the front tires being greater than the slip angle of the rear tires.

Un-Sprung Mass:
Typically considered as the mass between the road and the suspension springs.

Wheel Offset:
The distance between the wheel centerline and the wheel to hub mounting surface, when vied from the top of the vehicle, typically expressed in millimeters positive or negative. A positive wheel offset is when the distance measured from the wheel centerline extends away from the chassis. A negative wheel offset is when the distance measured from the wheel centerline extends towards the chassis.

Yaw:
The rotation of the vehicle's body around its center point when viewed from the top of the vehicle. When a vehicle enters a turn or makes a sudden lane change, it experiences a change in yaw. This change in yaw (yaw rate) can be used to determine if the vehicle is experiencing understeer or oversteer.